The Vagabond Spirit of Poetry

The Vagabond Spirit of Poetry

Edward Clarke

iff BOOKS

Winchester, UK
Washington, USA

First published by iff Books, 2014
iff Books is an imprint of John Hunt Publishing Ltd., Laurel House, Station Approach, Alresford, Hants, SO24 9JH, UK
office1@jhpbooks.net
www.johnhuntpublishing.com
www.iff-books.com

For distributor details and how to order please visit the 'Ordering' section on our website.

ISBN: 978 1 78279 370 0

A CIP catalogue record for this book is available from the British Library.

Design: Lee Nash

Printed and bound by CPI Group (UK) Ltd, Croydon, CR0 4YY

CONTENTS

Acknowledgements

The author has tried, in quoting copyright material, to abide by the conventions governing 'fair dealing'.

For different kinds of support and conversation, I would like to thank Tommy Allen, Jerome Boyd-Maunsell, Terence Brown, Anthony Caleshu, David and Sherille Clarke, Philip Coleman and Niamh NicGhabhann, Jonathan Creasy, Ralph Dennison, Ned Denny, Alexander Fiske-Harrison, Steve France, Naomi Freud, Nicola Gardini, Alex Goodwin, Emma, Paul, Elliot, Thomas and Rosa Griffin, Ernest Hilbert, John Hunt, Lee Jenkins, Francis Leneghan, Enrico Magnabosco and Dariel Bogliolo, Stephen Matterson, Dan Mitchell, Ines Molinaro, Louise Nelstrop, Bernard O'Donoghue, Robin Powley, Huw Roberts, Bartholomew Ryan, Paul Sinclair, Paul, Susan and Polly Saville, Malcolm Skene, Denise Smith, Tara Stubbs, Kate Watson, and especially Francesca Magnabosco and Ludovico Magnabosco-Clarke.

Note on Texts

I have quoted poets from modern editions of their works that keep original spelling and punctuation. Unless otherwise indicated, quotations from long poems or illuminated books, provided with book, canto or plate, and stanza or line, numbering, are taken from Homer 2003, Hesiod 2006-7, Virgil 1999-2000, Ovid 1904, Shantideva 2006, Dante 1996-2011, Spenser 1912, Milton 2007b, Pope 2005, Akenside 2000, Cowper 1971, Blake 2004, Wordsworth 2009, and Tennyson 1894. Shakespeare is quoted from Herbert Farjeon's edition of *The Complete Works* (1953); act, scene and line numbering, as well as the titles of plays, are from the 'The Globe Edition' (1891), allowing readers to find quotations easily in any *Complete Works*. Unless otherwise stated, Bible citations are from the King James Version: 1611 Edition (2010). Page numbers are given for quotations from all other works, which are listed in the Bibliography.

Personal Polemical Prologue

Indolence, industry and quick intuition

Between 11th and 13th July 1798 the day had come for William Wordsworth: 'when I again repose | Here, under this dark sycamore' (2009: 1. 372). The indolent poet was in his late twenties and on a walking tour up and down the Wye Valley, which divides Wales and England, whiling away the time between an unemployed season in a rented country mansion and a planned trip to Germany. He was probably wearing striped pantaloons. A younger admirer remembered him earlier that year dressed 'according to the *costume* of that unconstrained period', making 'havoc of the half of a Cheshire cheese', priding himself in his '"knowledge of the good things of this life"' (Hazlitt 1982: 58-9). With a mediocre degree from Cambridge and no career or fortune to speak of, Wordsworth was enjoying high summer. He was taking things slowly.

Who now reposes? Who has the time? Judging from the lists of quotations under the word in the *Oxford English Dictionary*, people were happily reposing in different ways from the sixteenth century up until about 1914, and then the verb falls out of circulation. Perhaps the First World War took away our repose. Can it be that since the beginning of the twentieth century we have known little cessation from work? Things have speeded up. 'Repose' is far too antiquated a word for the modern world. To repose is to lie down in rest, in perfect idleness against a tree, for example. Only the dead now seem to get away with reposing. We have forgotten that to repose is also to recover from and recharge, as one of Wordsworth's favourite eighteenth-century poets, William Cowper, well knew: day-dreaming by a winter's fire while a snow storm brews outside, ''Tis thus the understanding takes repose | In indolent vacuity of thought, | And sleeps and is refresh'd' (*The Task*, IV. 296-8).

It is precisely such refreshing repose that is taken away from Macbeth and Banquo, after their encounter with the witches, in that most prophetic of Shakespeare's plays. 'Good repose the while', wishes Macbeth, the night that he will kill the king, to the friend that he will later have murdered. 'Thankes Sir: the like to you', wishes Banquo back (*Macbeth*, II. i. 29-30). The dramatic irony of this short interchange is savage: once Banquo has been dispatched to his ultimate repose his ghost will not let Macbeth rest until he too dies. Of all Shakespeare's characters, Macbeth finds the least repose in this world; as soon as Banquo leaves him to go to bed, he will have his 'fatall Vision' (II. i. 36) of a dagger. Later on he is at once scared, exhilarated and caught up by his play's acceleration of 'Time' that 'anticipat'st my dread exploits' (IV. i. 144). Macbeth's world is suddenly speeded-up when he becomes King; he thinks that 'Time' performs actions before we have time to act: 'The flighty purpose never is o're-tooke | Unless the deed go with it' (IV. i. 145-6), that is, an intention must be carried out instantly or it will be too late. The frightening thing is that these days we are living in Macbeth's castle, which I see as a prophetic emblem of our industrialized world. Macbeth is an apocalyptic multitasker, plagued by stressful thoughts about the future. Like him we have lost our repose in a Hell of our own making.

I must confess that I awoke in the middle of the night to write these paragraphs, plagued by stressful thoughts about the day's tasks. At least writing about slowness and poetry helps me to gain some composure and embrace that which Wallace Stevens named 'the object of || The hum of thoughts evaded in the mind' (1954: 388). I have begun writing this book in a state of mild anxiety, fitting it in as a task among too many others, but my project is to discover how imagination, enlightened by reposeful reverie, puts reason to work in a divine, rather than a merely human, manner.

For years now Milan Kundera's questions at the beginning of his novel *Slowness* have echoed around my imagination:

> Why has the pleasure of slowness disappeared? Ah, where have they gone, the amblers of yesteryear? Where have they gone, those loafing heroes of folk song, those vagabonds who roam from one mill to another and bed down under the stars? Have they vanished along with footpaths, with grasslands and clearings, with nature? There is a Czech proverb that describes their easy indolence by a metaphor: 'They are gazing at God's windows.' A person gazing at God's windows is not bored; he is happy. In our world, indolence has turned into having nothing to do, which is a completely different thing: a person with nothing to do is frustrated, bored, is constantly searching for the activity he lacks. (1996: 4-5)

Macbeth was bored perhaps, but, ambitiously searching for the political activity he lacked, he ended up despairing about 'To morrow, and to morrow, and to morrow' (V. v. 19). Wordsworth is productively indolent, reposing on the precious breast of visionary creativity. How can we become loafing heroes in our frenetic modern world? How can we find the time to gaze at God's windows?

W. B. Yeats called William Blake's *Songs of Innocence,* which Blake illustrated himself, 'illuminated missals of song in which every page is a window open in Heaven'. Such windows are:

> open not as in the days of Noah for the outpouring of the flood 'of time and space,' but that we may look into 'the golden age' and 'the imagination that liveth for ever,' and talk with those who dwell there by 'Poetry, Painting, and Music, the three powers in man of conversing with Paradise which the flood did not sweep away.' (Blake 2002: xxix)

Yeats is quoting from Blake's 'A Vision of The Last Judgment' (2008: 559). The slow and indolent art of reading poems allows us to gaze at God's windows, to converse with characters in 'Paradise'.

Slowness is not just about being less fast. In fact, the peculiar slowness that poetry can demand of its readers preludes a certain kind of inner acceleration. At that moment we are gathered by the 'intensest rendezvous', and feel the quickening of 'A light, a power, the miraculous influence', as Stevens recognizes in a late poem called 'Final Soliloquy of the Interior Paramour'. Such intuitive conversations are when 'We say God and the imagination are one…' They come swiftly after we have slowed down for a spell, by resting, for example, 'as in a room', or in the clearing, of a poem (1954: 524).

Who are the loafing heroes of folk song? I think of the ballad supposedly 'compos-ed by Spencer the Rover', a man with money problems who left his young family to rove around Yorkshire:

> Till being weary of rambling, he sat down to rest
> At the foot of yon' mountain there runs a clear flowing fountain
> Of bread and cold water himself did refresh.
>
> With the night fast approaching, to the woods he resorted
> With wood, vine and ivy his bed for to make
> But he dreamt about sighing, lamenting and crying
> Go home to your family and rambling forsake. (see Roud 2012: 210)

By slowing down, even bedding down, under the stars, Spencer the Rover finds the strength to return to the 'prittle prattling stories' of his children, which also help 'to drive care away'. His indolent loafing, shunning care for a spell, which may seem merely irresponsible to some, actually leads to a kind of mystical experience in the wood, a dream from which he can return to the everyday world refreshed to accept his responsibilities as a father. Such are the beneficent effects of slow indolence, and I would argue that reading a poem allows us to embark in miniature on a journey similar to that of Spencer the Rover. A poem takes us temporarily out of our everyday world, but we return from such an excursion renewed to face practical challenges; patiently to act again, not as 'a poore Player | That struts and frets his houre upon the Stage' (*Macbeth*, V. v. 24-5), but feeling 'A presence that disturbs me with the joy | Of elevated thoughts' (Wordsworth 2009: 1. 374-5).

Some of Shakespeare's finest characters are loafing heroes who seem to have strolled straight out of folk song. The fantastic rogue Autolycus, for example, first enters the very late play, *The Winter's Tale,* while improvising a song from which Macbeth would do well to learn. Autolycus tells us that he once served the Prince, wearing a fine livery of velvet, 'but now I am out of service':

But shall I go mourne for that (my deere)
the pale Moone shines by night:
And when I wander here, and there
I then do most go right. (IV. iii. 15-8)

We have happened upon another ballad full of sense, another hero who knows all about the pleasures of slowness. A modern editor of *The Winter's Tale* offers an almost cynical gloss of Autolycus' lines: 'But shall I worry about that [i.e. having lost my job with the prince]? On moonlight nights when I go where I like [and steal what I can] then I am living the life which is the one for me'; 'to travel without a destination is the vagabond's principle' (Shakespeare 2006: 81). But such an interpretation pays attention merely to the worldly meaning of Autolycus' song. It is too hasty a reading. We should remember that Shakespeare's lines face God's windows as much as they face the world. And in that case we might try and read him as a vagabond would. Such is the hope of this book: that we can learn to read great poetry as visionary vagabonds might.

Autolycus is not just singing about the pleasures of the life of a vagabond; he is affirming the virtues of slowness for us all. His name means 'the wolf himself' and I believe that Shakespeare speaks through this character to affirm, as Robert Graves will in the twentieth century, that 'The function of poetry is religious invocation of the Muse; its use is the experience of mixed exaltation and horror that her presence excites', which, as we have seen, Stevens describes as 'the miraculous influence' (1999: 10): the inner acceleration of the 'intensest rendezvous' with the 'Interior Paramour'. The Muse is symbolized by 'the pale Moone': Autolycus' song today can function as a warning to us that our commitment to the fast-paced 'industrial machine' prevents us from rendering the slow and whole-hearted service that the White Goddess requires, if we are each truly to be quickened from within, rather than merely possessed by our demons.

To be possessed by demons today, ironically, is not to believe in the supernatural cause of everything, or what Blake called 'Imagination' (*Jerusalem*, Plate 5. 20), the ground of all creation: that 'divine force' (1968: sig. B4^{v}) that Sir Philip Sidney understood inheres also in poetry. Blake thought of disbelief as demonic: we are possessed by demons unwittingly when we only affirm the reality of the world that we can see around us and deny the existence of the eternal realms of 'Imagination'.

When I talk of the supernatural in this book I mean that which is above nature and which rules nature. In Apuleius' *Metamorphoses* this primordial power reveals itself in visionary dream, and comes as a response to Lucius' desperate prayer to be transformed from the shape of an ass. Apuleius calls this divine force Isis but she says herself:

> I am Nature, the universal Mother, mistress of all the elements, primordial child of time, sovereign of all things spiritual, queen of the dead, queen also of the immortals, the single manifestation of all gods and goddesses that are. My

> nod governs the shining heights of Heaven, the wholesome sea-breezes, the lamentable silences of the world below. Though I am worshipped in many aspects, known by countless names, and propitiated with all manner of different rites, yet the whole round earth venerates me. (1964: 271)

That which is 'sovereign of all things spiritual' is also 'Nature' because, as Blake understood, 'every thing that lives is Holy' (2004: 133). A modern scientist would argue that such a statement is meaningless: life is just one way that matter can behave, which we can observe and quantify. Rational atheism would deprive man of experience of the holy. But, as Kathleen Raine emphasizes, Lucius' mixed feelings of joy and terror and wonder in the presence of Isis '*are* experiences which fall within the range of our humanity' (1991: 28). Blake would have understood that when the ass prays to Isis, he is waking up from the slumber of materialism to Imagination, 'the land of life', and his eventual transformation back to a man, effected by Isis, symbolizes this process. In poems like Stevens' 'Final Soliloquy of the Interior Paramour' Isis shows us on earth that 'the human Imagination is the divine in man' as it engages with reality: 'Eternity is the Imaginative vision; and Imagination is "the Saviour"' (Raine 1991: 23 and 28).

Luckily for us, poetry is littered with loafing heroes from whom we can learn about the supernatural cause of everything. In Theocritus' seventh Idyll, written in the third century BC, we encounter Lycidas who appears to be a goatherd, dressed as he is in a shaggy goat's fleece smelling of new-made rennet; his ancient shirt fastened with a broad belt, a curved stick of wild olive wood in his right hand. The speaker of the poem, Simichidas, who may or may or not be Theocritus himself, on the way to a harvest festival, overtook this goatherd, and Lycidas, quietly, broadly, and with a twinkling eye grinned at him; 'laughter touched his lip as he spoke':

> 'Where are you off to, Simichidas, in the noonday heat,
> Bustling along, even when the lizard sleeps in the wall,
> And tomb-haunting larks look to find their rest?
> Such haste – have you invited yourself to dinner somewhere,
> Or to sample a townsman's wine jar? At the pace you're going
> The pebbles sing as they spurt from under your boots.' (2008: 25)

Lycidas' sudden appearance and charmed smile suggest divinity; his very name, which shares the same root of the Greek word for wolf with Autolycus, may also evoke *lykios*, an epithet of Apollo, the god of medicine, music and poetry. The encounter is certainly a kind of awakening for the hurrying Simichidas who slows down to exchange songs with Lycidas. When he gives Simichidas his olive stick at the end we realize that the poem records a poetic initiation: such are the rewards of slowing down, the loafing wayfarer you fall in with may provide you with life-changing insights and gifts.

Virgil takes up the name Lycidas a couple of centuries later in one of his own pastoral poems, the poignant ninth *Eclogue*. Lycidas is here another loafer by the wayside and a pastoral poet. He asks of a passer-by: '"Where are you headed, Moeris? Into town?"' Moeris, a tenant farmer, is herding his new landlord's goats to market, but he is deeply upset because this outsider has just told him that he will have to leave his farm. It seems that there was a dispute in which the poet Menalcas, who may or may not be Virgil, failed to secure their land against the claims of soldiers. As Lycidas walks with Moeris they talk of, and sing snatches from, old songs: '"There was something I heard you singing by yourself | One night when the sky was clear"', remembers Lycidas. '"Age robs us of everything, of our very mind"', replies Moeris; '"Many a time I remember as a boy | Serenading the slow sun down to rest, | But nowadays I'm forgetting song after song"'. Lycidas suggests that they stop before a tomb and sing, but Moeris declines the offer: '"That's enough of that, young fellow. We've a job to do"' (Heaney 2001: 33-4).

When we are consumed by business we forget old songs; as Virgil registers at the end of this eclogue, there is always a tension between the 'divine force' of poetry and worldly cares, mundane haste: in this world the soul is already soiled by that which Lao tzu would have called dust. Moeris, who has begun to sound a bit like a gentle prototype of Macbeth, might have done better to stop and sing for a while in the country before pressing on to town. Sadly we have inherited his unease and largely forgotten, like him, the old songs. Virgil's poem makes me ask, how can we change our attitude to time? Does time only bear all away, anticipating our exploits? When we slow down, can we discover instead a moment in what was a busy day that renovates all the moments of that day?

When John Milton composed an elegy for a dead university acquaintance, Edward King, he decided to rename him Lycidas. If this poem, called 'Lycidas', is at all a window open in Heaven, then Milton was lamenting at the same time the passing of the loafing hero in the modern age:

Yet once more, O ye Laurels, and once more
Ye Myrtles brown, with Ivy never-sear,
I com to pluck your Berries harsh and crude,
And with forc'd fingers rude,
Shatter your leaves before the mellowing year.
Bitter constraint, and sad occasion dear,
Compels me to disturb your season due:
For *Lycidas* is dead, dead ere his prime
Young *Lycidas*, and hath not left his peer:
Who would not sing for *Lycidas*? he knew
Himself to sing, and build the lofty rhyme.
He must not flote upon his watry bear

Unwept and welter to the parching wind,
Without the meed of som melodious tear. (2009: 74-5)

By employing the name Lycidas, Milton is deliberately recalling Theocritus' seventh Idyll and Virgil's ninth Eclogue. He has not chosen this name at random from bucolic or pastoral poetry. This half-divine poet-rustic who can be found suddenly by the wayside emblematizes something our busy urban culture all too often overlooks: 'But O the heavy change, now thou art gon, | Now thou art gon, and never must return!' Milton laments. 'Lycidas' bewails the death of a particular person. Does the poem also provide us with a modern version of an old-fashioned kind of poetic initiation? If we slow down on occasion, then we just might find Lycidas again, and our encounter with this loafing hero can lead to poetic wisdom; we recover knowledge of man's godlike and quickening powers of imagination. Such encounters often take place within poems if we are slow enough and attentive readers.

It is significant in Milton's elegy that Lycidas has drowned. Edward King had in fact drowned in the Irish Seas in 1637. But Milton would have understood the symbolic significance for King's second or spiritual self, Lycidas: to drown in the sea is to be caught up in this sea of time and space, this material world, the flood that swept away Paradise, which is the true domain of our immortal soul. This spiritual sense of the poem seems at odds with its literal sense. In 'Lycidas', Milton is ostensibly lamenting the death of a friend by drowning. But, if the figure of Lycidas can be thought of as an emblem of man's immortal soul, as well as a poetic name for Edward King, then Milton's poem is also a lamentation for the passing of any soul into generation, our world on earth, which is symbolized by the sea. We are drowned in the sea of time and space, from which King as Lycidas has been saved, ironically, by drowning. In fact, such a reading of the poem, finding its hidden spiritual sense, should provide us with solace. Milton is saying that our birth is a kind of death and our death a kind of birth: a release from this death-like state back into eternity.

The poem itself provides a way for each of us to recognize the immortality of the soul on earth because, as Blake knew, poetry, like painting and music, is one power in man of 'conversing with Paradise which the flood did not Sweep away'. 'Lycidas' provides each reader with the opportunity to recover 'Imaginative vision' because it would speak to us from eternity. The poem's spiritual significance as an elegy for the immortal soul on earth contains its historical significance as an elegy for a dead friend. Blake would have understood that our conversation with 'Paradise' is the human imagination recognizing that it is itself 'the divine in man', and poems like 'Lycidas' can provide the time and place for such conversation: 'as in a room' we find ourselves readied for the 'intensest rendezvous'.

Milton imagines his poem as if sung by an 'uncouth Swain' idling away a whole day in the countryside:

> And now the Sun had stretch'd out all the hills,
> And now was dropt into the Western bay;
> At last he rose, and twitch'd his Mantle blew:
> To morrow to fresh woods, and Pastures new. (2009: 80)

Wordsworth, reposing underneath a sycamore at the beginning of his poem 'Tintern Abbey', knew very well that he was joining a long line of literary loafers. This book will settle down with some of them to ease into quietly productive conversations about poetry. It also looks to 'fresh woods' and 'Pastures new' and wonders about slowing down and reading poetry in our modern age. Like a loafing figure by the roadside a poem can waylay each of us on the road to business in town, it can take us out of our worldly concerns for a spell, in order to return us to our path, refreshed to notice new things, to deal differently with others in the world.

Blake made his prophetic poem, *Milton*, to correct Milton's errors, by opening his precursor's poems on to a new apprehension of Heaven. It is an attempt to read Milton as I have just interpreted 'Lycidas'. At the climax of *Milton* we are told:

> There is a Moment in each Day that Satan cannot find
> Nor can his Watch Fiends find it, but the Industrious find
> This Moment & it multiply. & when it once is found
> It renovates every Moment of the Day if rightly placed[.]
> (*Milton*, Plate 35. 42-5)

How do we reconcile indolence with industry? *In-dolentia* is a Latin word, invented by Cicero, meaning freedom from pain; indolence is a state of rest or a love of ease, which is often now derided as mere laziness. Industry, on the other hand, has been understood since the sixteenth century as a virtue comprehending both study and diligence; it requires habitual employment in some useful work, although now it seems more like the vice of capitalism. These two states seem incongruous. Yet Blake's 'Industrious', who find 'a Moment in each Day that Satan cannot find', partake of a special kind of indolence. Such indolence helps us to find the right kind of industry; conversely such industry opens out the day to radiant and productive indolence. Industrious indolence and indolent industry: let us think of these oxymoronic states as the day-dreaming that is the necessary prelude to sustained imaginative work and that patient and joyous labour itself.

Slowness does not preclude work, but finds for us our work; it allows us to become receptive and creative rather than merely busy like Satan and his Watch Fiends, who are a Blakeian version of the demoniac Macbeth and the servants whom he employs as spies. Macbeth's busy kind of industry leads to the 'Industrial Revolution', Blake's indolent kind of industry leads out of that labyrinth to 'Heavens gate, | Built in Jerusalem's wall' (*Jerusalem*, Plate 77). Modern or Macbethian industry puts many employees, in especially poorer countries, in a lot of pain; the industry of the indolent provides potential release from that pain, if we could but take the time to read their work.

For Blake, Satan is selfhood. Industry born of indolence allows us to get over ourselves in order to apprehend that which reason alone cannot comprehend: that 'God and the imagination are one'. Both the truly indolent and the truly industrious gaze at God's windows; each, in its authentic state, is the converse side of the same coin. Anyone's everyday self is very easily distracted and would busily employ itself on its 'way to' what Macbeth calls 'dusty death', the road along which Simichidas rushes, kicking up the pebbles with his dusty boots as he goes. This book invites your everyday self to pause for a moment; it would waylay you, so that you might converse with the vagabond spirit of poetry.

By slowing down to a stop temporarily today, even just to glance at this book, you have already discovered (whether you know it or not) that 'bright eternal Self' (Yeats and Swami 1970: 135), the friend within: you are face to face with Lycidas by the wayside. Such an indolent encounter can make a reader industrious in the right way and such repose is found each day by truly industrious souls who understand the worth of great poetry. Renovation comes to those prepared to read poems slowly. As Wordsworth jotted in a notebook in February 1798, a few months before composing 'Tintern Abbey', 'there is a holy indolence | Compared to which our best activity | Is oftimes deadly bane' (1979a: 115) and as King Lear's doctor understood, 'Our foster Nurse of Nature, is repose' (IV. iv. 12). If you are willing to embrace the slow and poetic mode of being in the world, then you can reorient an otherwise overly rational, perhaps even baneful or Macbethian, existence. You will also come to a far deeper understanding of the poems themselves.

Slowness does not preclude swiftness: a great virtue of poetry is that it admits the acceleration of intuition. The celerity of poetry is exhilarating. It apprehends more than we can comprehend even in speeded-up terrestrial time. As Philip Pullman says of fairy tales, travelling fast and light, the greatest poems 'are perfect examples of what you do need and what you don't' (2012: xiv-xv); they burn brightly, in 'a Moment' of eternity, when every word counts. Such supernatural speed is the reward of taking the time to read poems in the middle of today's mundane bustle. Anyone's encounter with Lycidas by the wayside involves a momentary quickening of the heart, a sudden recognition within of something unexpected without, which will change gradually the way in which we live in the world. At the end of everyday time, poetry returns us 'In a moment, in the twinckling of an eye' (1 Corinthians 15. 52) to imaginative consciousness, which will always have outstripped our corruptible business in town.

Where are you off to?

An uncompromising and playful voice by the side of your career asks: 'who are you? Where are you going? Do you think that you are on the right path? What are you doing with your life? When was the last time you stilled your mundane thoughts to understand the way things are? When was the last time you read some soul-stirring poetry?' Bustling common-sense replies: 'what time can I possibly have for that kind of thing when I also have a job and a family and an iPad? I've got too much going on right now. We all had to study some poems at school, but why should I have read anything like that since then? And as for meditating on nothing, is there any time on a Monday morning to become so fully awake?' The voice does not go away.

You may be studying English literature at university, and even there it's very easy not to bother reading Milton, Shakespeare, or indeed any poet at all. Why would you, when you can deconstruct Thomas Pynchon or fail to understand Michel Foucault? You may teach English literature in a school, and no doubt you could successfully avoid poetry most of the time. If you are a professor of literature, you may pass up poetry altogether, and even if you don't, you may be more interested in historical contexts, psychoanalytic literary criticism or cultural theory than prosody and soul-making. You may be an eminent philosopher or a distinguished scientist, a lawyer or a social worker, an actor or a business man, a politician or a refuse-collector, you may even be an artist, and perhaps you haven't read a poem carefully for years. There are many highly educated professionals out there who no longer have, or never really had, much interest in poems, and many highly intelligent non-professionals too.

Why should we be so largely indifferent to poetry today? Some pundits, like the poet Don Paterson, describe how the Modernists took poetry away from the common man after the First World War. Reacting against sentimental but popular late Romantic English poems, two erudite but supercilious Americans, Ezra Pound and T. S. Eliot, started writing a harder kind of poetry. Careful to use no superfluous words, they nonetheless indulged in making numerous obscure references in their free verse. In many ways, the argument runs, this was a good thing. They helped to purge contemporary poetry of a lot of nostalgic nonsense. They were determined to be accurate about their feelings on paper as they discovered a new urban idiom. But their poems can be still quite unappealing outside of the classroom. If you do not live in an ivory tower, can you really be bothered to spend hours not noticing allusions to texts that you haven't read, in order to half-understand a poem that merely describes the terrible state of the world today? Luckily for Eliot *The Waste Land* appeared just when the study of English literature at university was taking off and it has been championed by English professors ever since.

Now, according to this argument, a myth has grown outside

of academia that poetry is too difficult for the likes of us: if I need comfort or guidance, I'm hardly going to turn to a poem, as my grandmother might have done. Academics, on the other hand, have become so entangled in the intricacies of history and theory, a labyrinth of research, that most of them miss the original function of poetry. But even to offer this explanation of why poetry is now, as Paterson says, a 'marginal art form' (Wroe 2006) is to risk becoming part of the problem.

I take a much slower and larger view. Milton asked his Muse, in the late seventeenth century, over half-way through his biblical epic poem, *Paradise Lost*, 'still govern thou my Song, | *Urania*, and fit audience find, though few' (VII. 30-1). Perhaps certain kinds of poets have only ever expected a small proportion of the population to be their audience. Then again, Milton had just acknowledged that he had 'fall'n on evil dayes' (VII. 25). His days might well have seemed evil since he was at that time in political exile in his own country and he was blind. Yeats and Blake, two poets influenced strongly by Neoplatonic wisdom and extremely well-read in esoteric literature, would have understood that Milton also meant the modern age in general. Since the late seventeenth century, poetry and its fit audience have declined still further.

By 1931, as Yeats well knew, 'all is changed, that high horse riderless, | Though mounted in that saddle Homer rode | Where the swan drifts upon a darkening flood' (1950: 276). The swan is man's soul, the darkening flood, the sea of time and space: our life on earth at the moment. The high horse of great poetry, the 'flying Steed' that Milton also rode (see *Paradise Lost*, VII. 12-20), lacks a rider today because we are at the end of an epoch that was already hastening to its finishing-post by the late seventeenth century. At the beginning of that epoch, in ancient societies, poetry had a more central role. Can it be that, at its end, in our decayed, decadent, materialist culture, a new reality is born, that a new rider can learn to sit in that saddle Homer rode?

Today we are experiencing the winding down of one period in a process of change. I find myself in a late phase, preceding a new one that has already begun, in what the ancients thought of as the 'Great Year', a vast astronomical cycle that contains many historical epochs. Blake restored vivifying knowledge of this way of reckoning time to our modern age in his poem 'The Mental Traveller', which Yeats elaborated with his model of two interlocking gyres in his abstruse treatise *A Vision*. As Raine has pointed out: 'Plato also sees history as a perpetual movement between two poles; sometimes God conducts the universe, and controls its revolutions; at another time He leaves it to its own devices' (2002: 60-1). For a long while now, since before the time of Homer, we have been left to our own devices, during one epoch of the 'Great Year'. The spring that God had wound is now uncoiling itself, and with increasing rapidity in our modern age, performing, as Plato says, 'many myriads of retrograde revolutions'.

We live according to the consequences of such uncoiling. Swearing by capitalism, democracy, reason and science, we are all the while cheerfully ignorant about supernatural powers that hide themselves in great poetry. But we can learn to read the most potent poems that have come down to us so that we trace unexpected insights. New poems and interpretation may change the meaning of the canon, and I would argue that our older poems are to be seen as remade by younger ones, so that they function as divine prompts, like Lycidas by the wayside. If we act on their revealed suggestions then we can learn to wind the spring of the next age ourselves: we begin to awake from our rational and materialist slumber by acknowledging that God is within the human imagination.

You may not believe in God. Our age no longer takes the supernatural for granted. You may long for faith, but feel reluctant to go to church every Sunday. I contend that the greatest poetry can make us apprehend that God, the centre of religious celebration, whatever we call that nothingness or darkness, incomprehensible and vast in its own being, is a force within man. Such apprehension means that the swan no longer 'drifts upon a darkening flood' but mounts into the sky. Rather than be moved passively along our current, materialist perceptions of the world, along the dusty road to business in town, this book asks of poetry, suddenly and slowly, how each soul might rise to Wordsworth's finely expressed feeling that 'we are greater than we know' (2009: 3. 363).

I have come to recognize that each of us contains vast cycles of history. Our present transition from one phase to another in the 'Great Year' is dependent on the individual discovering a greater self within, on her becoming responsible enough to make our soul. I write this book out of a conviction that poetry is much more powerful and useful than our existing culture admits. Certain poems can help each of us to change together our dark time. In fact, the spring is already being wound but most of us do not know it yet.

All of this sounds terribly strenuous, but the wonderful thing about reading poetry is that it is in essence a pleasurable activity, even before you've learned the basics. I must admit that I enjoy reading poems and this book takes time to enlarge my experience of some of them by sharing my delight, by teaching some of those basics. It may take some time to change the world, but poetry can immediately quicken your powers of intuition, if you can learn to catch it by an instinct, to catch up to its sudden accelerations and transformations.

I'm going to be quoting sometimes-longish passages of poetry, using their original spelling and punctuation. Please do not be put off. I hope that my book proves how we can allow texts to mean more, by retaining original forms of words, rather than by modernizing them. Original spelling is not, after all, an obstacle to comprehension of my quotations, and at least strange looking words may make you re-read their contexts, even if you know them well. I quote from some of my favourite moments in English literature and they deserve to be read, 'and againe, and againe', as Shakespeare's first editors advised we read his plays (1953: 1. xlix). My quotations are also signposts. All of the poets that I refer to should be given more time than my book can afford them, and if you consult the Bibliography you will be guided to the best editions of their poems.

My method in this book is to practice what Stevens called 'pure explication de texte' (1996: 793). Such careful, scrupulous interpretation of poems is carried out in order to learn from poets how to go about making our soul in the modern world. My main motivation is that poetry matters. It is of central importance to our culture and we endanger ourselves when we forget that. No other art form brings back messages from the silence that is at the heart of our being by using the half-material something that makes us human.

Poetry reaches that which music, painting, sculpture and conceptual art cannot. We may be made out of earth but we are formed by language. You may use words to order a pint or to inquire about a masticating juicer, but poets dispose words, in lines that make you pause at their ends, to help you lose yourself to find that greater self that reposes within.

The book's scope

At the entrance to Purgatory, in Dante's *Divine Comedy*, the guardian angel inscribed seven *P*s upon the pilgrim's forehead with the point of his sword, saying 'See that you wash these wounds, when you are within' (*Purgatorio*, IX. 113-4). The *P*s could stand for *Peccatum* (sin), *Plaga* (wound), and *Penitentia* (penitence): the soul now advances to active purgation.

Like Dante the pilgrim I feel that I have undertaken this book with seven *P*s on my forehead. My work moves me, and quite often I am lazily reluctant, towards expiation: it marks me out as among 'the men that sigh, and that cry for all the abominations'

(Ezekiel 9. 4).

Since I am such a marked man, you could say that this book begins where Joseph Campbell leaves off, with 'personal despair':

> It is not society that is to guide and save the creative hero, but precisely the reverse. And so every one of us shares the supreme ordeal – carries the cross of the redeemer – not in the bright moments of his tribes great victories, but in the silences of his personal despair. (1993: 391)

The poets through the generations have always been ahead of their communities, and they are ahead of ours now. The reader of poetry can be a hero if he slows down and dares to heed that which calls from out of it. That divine power reposing by the wayside who grins 'quietly, broadly, and with a twinkling eye' at our bustling everyday selves can change suddenly and slowly the course of our busy lives. Our guardian spirits reside in poems and they would bring our souls to crisis. Ultimately poets cannot help us in that state of crisis on the road to self-knowledge, as Wordsworth well knew, but they can at least direct us to a point of self-revelation. Self-revelation is divine revelation: when 'We say God and the imagination are one…' That is something I also believe. You may discover for yourself the supernatural correspondence of poems, or you may not, that is your concern. I hope that you still enjoy this book either way.

Although, as you will see in the first chapter, I may disagree with Wordsworth's obsession with personal memory in *The Prelude*, my concerns in this book are the same as his in that poem – imagination, love and self-knowledge:

> Imagination having been our theme,
> So also hath that intellectual love,
> For they are each in each, and cannot stand

Dividually. – Here must thou be, O Man!
Strength to thyself; no Helper has thou here;
Here keepest thou thy individual state:
No other can divide with thee this work[.] (*1805 Prelude,* XIII. 185-91)

When we confront this abyss, which is not solipsism, but an apprehension of a greater and at once terrifying and supporting power within, we discover rejuvenated relations in the world. When we are guided towards this divine power, we develop more profound and fructifying relations with our literature. As Wordsworth proclaims: 'joy to him, | O joy to him who here hath sown, hath laid | Here the foundations of his future years' (*1805 Prelude,* XIII. 197-9)!

It was said of my last book that I do 'not hesitate to deal in the spiritual dimensions opened up' (Clarke 2012: back cover) by my chosen poets. Let me hesitate at the opening of this book. I believe that if we are to get on the right path to spiritual understanding, to lay 'the foundations of [our] future years', then we must find or continue with our work in this world. We should not abandon our society. My work is the teaching of English literature. Writing is essential to that activity: as Bacon said, '"reading makes a full man, conversation a ready man, and writing an exact man"' (Johnson 2000: 269). But getting on the right path allows one to question one's mundane activities. The words of Rumi echo in my head:

> Concentrate upon spirituality as you will – it will shun you if you are unworthy. Write about it, boast of it, comment upon it – it will decline to benefit you; it will flee. But, if it sees your concentration, it may come to your hand, like a trained bird. Like the peacock, it will not sit in an unworthy place. (Shah 1977: 125)

My hope in writing this book is my concentration and yours. I do not mean merely to comment upon spirituality, but to call to it. Like Kierkegaard, I write 'without authority': for me the writing of this book constitutes part of 'my own upbringing and development' (1998: 12).

Wordsworth's 'Tintern Abbey', which was begun while he was reposing under that 'dark sycamore' on his 1798 tour of the Wye Valley, ends as a kind of meditative prayer, 'for thy sake'. At its climax the poet does not regret the passing of the animal pleasures of his undergraduate days, the period of his life, five years before, when he had first visited the ruins of Tintern Abbey:

for such loss, I would believe,
Abundant recompence. For I have learned
To look on nature not as in the hour
Of thoughtless youth, but hearing oftentimes
The still, sad music of humanity,
Nor harsh nor grating, though of ample power
To chasten and subdue. And I have felt
A presence that disturbs me with the joy
Of elevated thoughts; a sense sublime
Of something far more deeply interfused,
Whose dwelling is the light of setting suns,
And the round ocean, and the living air,
And the blue sky, and in the mind of man,
A motion and a spirit, that impels
All thinking things, all objects of all thought,
And rolls through all things. (2009: 1. 374-5)

I've recently been re-reading a book by Thich Nhat Hanh called *The Miracle of Mindfulness*. It's really a series of letters written by an exiled Vietnamese Buddhist monk to those working in his homeland in the 1970s, offered as means to help them rebuild their country after the war there. The book has been published as a manual on meditation: it offers exercises for taking hold of one's breath to become fully conscious of the moment in which one lives; that 'Moment in each Day that Satan cannot find', 'that Renovates every Moment of the Day if rightly placed'. Thich Nhat Hanh would say that Wordsworth is mindful that you are in the universe and the universe is in you; measuring his steps along the Wye valley, he comes to compose the above lines with a half smile (see Thich Nhat Hanh 1991: 89-90).

It is very difficult to meditate and to empty one's mind. But it strikes me that reading a poem is one way of learning to take hold of one's breath and to reorganize one's relation to the world. The secular west lacks spiritual discipline and naturally turns to the east for help. But we have our own traditions and mysteries, our own ways of taking hold of breath. If we begin to inhabit the body of English poetry that we have inherited, by reciting poems and remembering them, we find that we have been provided with native exercises sufficient to apprehend that we are greater than we know. We come to apprehend with joy that 'age-long memoried' (Yeats 1980: 272) or 'bright eternal Self' that abides in any great poet's body of work. Raine explains:

> In Eastern civilizations some form of meditation is the norm of spiritual practise. For Blake art was such a practise and the arts are the channels through which visions of these 'eternal things displayed' are embodied and disseminated. 'Prayer is the study of Art. Praise is the practise of Art'. Prayer is receptive, praise active: the one must precede the other. (1991: 6)

In the following chapters we will read together many poems to contemplate 'eternal things displayed'.

These seven essays are each discrete, but also designed to be read in sequence as continuous chapters. We begin in the middle of things with Wordsworth, in order to invoke supernatural presences in poetry in Chapter 2. From Chapter 3 onwards we embark on a chronological journey through the English-speaking generations of poets, from Shakespeare to two of the greatest poets of the twentieth century, W. B. Yeats and Wallace Stevens. Inevitably, my attention to the pre-eminent British, Irish and American poets of the modern age, involves also a host of earlier poets, including especially Homer, Hesiod, Theocritus, Virgil and Ovid from the classical age, and Dante from the middle ages. As we take this journey together I aim to answer major complaints about poetry that I hear voiced by teenagers, students, strangers in pubs, highly intelligent but ironic friends and relatives, and even professors of English literature. You can think of the seven chapters of this book as offering exercises in slow reading so that life is accelerated by intuition.

Chapter 1

Wordsworth's Survival on Earth

Spots of time

Judging from our current obsessions with history, psychoanalysis and the lives of celebrities, most people today would probably half-agree with Wordsworth that:

> There are in our existence spots of time
> Which with distinct pre-eminence retain
> A fructifying virtue[.] (*1799 Prelude*, I. 288-90)

If we 'fly alongside' Victoria Beckham 'on her journey from lonely teenager', by reading her autobiography, then we learn about those moments that helped her become 'the star she is today' (2002: back cover). For Posh Spice, one significant spot of time was her early exposure to a line from the theme song to the movie *Fame* – 'I'm gonna live forever, I'm gonna learn how to fly' – from which,

> depressed
> By trivial occupations and the round
> Of ordinary intercourse,

family life, tap-dancing lessons, PR,

> [her] mind
> (Especially the imaginative power)
> [Was] nourished, and invisibly repaired.

The line from the song stayed with the young Victoria, nourishing her fantasies when she was depressed by the trivial occupations of ordinary life and stage school; it caused her vision of fame to fructify into the reality that was Posh Spice because, as Wordsworth understood,

> Such moments chiefly seem to have their date
> In our first childhood. (*1799 Prelude*, I. 290-6)

Nearly everyone now believes that childhood experience is of formative consequence. But why should Wordsworth be so inclusive about his even larger claims that 'spots of time' nourish creativity in adulthood? If my existence has any such pre-eminent spots, or memories, I am not sure how well they have retained a fructifying virtue to nourish my creative imagination today. In any case I do not think that we do well to obsess about them. Formative experience is a treacherous theme for a true poet. I believe that the worst kind of poetry is confessional: in my opinion, Robert Lowell, John Berryman and Sylvia Plath are depressingly limited and dangerously egotistical poets.

It could be argued that *The Prelude*, from which the above lines are taken, preludes the state of literature and our society today since it is a work concerned with the poet's own life. But Wordsworth did not think it appropriate to publish this autobiographical epic poem during his own lifetime (I will go into more detail about Wordsworth writing and revising *The Prelude* from 1798 onwards later in this chapter). He saw it only as the prelude to a greater kind of philosophical poem, which he was ultimately unable to write, and arguably because he sought the sources of his creativity in the wrong direction. By writing *The Prelude* Wordsworth by no means guaranteed his future creativity, he may even have destroyed it and indirectly invented the Spice Girls.

Inspiration does not come from our past. We will not find a solution to our problems by dwelling on childhood memories or even by simply recalling old books and ancient wisdom. In the words of James Hillman, *We've Had a Hundred Years of Psychotherapy – And the World's Getting Worse*. We've had over two hundred years of self-reflexive literature and philosophy and we can no longer help ourselves: consumed by self-obsessed poems, fast-ballooning novels, theoretical criticism, historicism and so-called reality television shows, man has lost sight of himself on the earth that he has polluted.

At my rampant worst I would rather go shopping online than know myself, let alone practice losing my everyday self to find that 'bright eternal Self' (Yeats and Swami 1970: 135) that dwells within and without. Closing Google for a spell, to focus on this challenging Word document, I ask, are there spots of time in poetry that have nothing to do with personal memory? How can these moments possibly renew our lives and our world? If such spots seem to come from out of the past, how can we make them of the future? How can poems help us to restore, by integrating, our impoverished inner soul and the largely ignored outer soul of our sick world?

Out damned spot

When I read Wordsworth's expression 'spots of time' I cannot help but think of the most famous 'spot' in English literature, the bloodstain that Lady Macbeth imagines on her hands:

> *Enter Lady, with a Taper*
> *Gentlewoman*: Lo you, here she comes: This is her very guise, and upon my life fast asleepe: observe her, stand close.
> *Doctor*: How came she by that light?
> *Gentlewoman:* Why it stood by her: she ha's light by her continually, 'tis her command.
> *Doctor*: You see her eyes are open.
> *Gentlewoman*: I but their sense are shut.
> *Doctor*: What is it she do's now?
> Looke how she rubbes her hands.

Gentlewoman: It is an accustom'd action with her, to seeme thus washing her hands: I have knowne her continue in this a quarter of an houre.
Lady Macbeth: Yet heere's a spot.
Doctor: Heark, she speaks, I will set downe what comes from her, to satisfie my remembrance the more strongly.
Lady Macbeth: Out damned spot: out I say. One: Two: Why then 'tis time to doo't: Hell is murky. (V. i. 22-41)

As well as being a small discolouring mark, a spot is a moral stain, a stigma or disgrace. The doctor is taking dictation from the sleep-walking Lady Macbeth as I imagine a modern day psychotherapist would take notes when talking to a reclining patient who is relating her formative spots of time or memories. We have become Lady Macbeth: most of us are sleep-walking through a dark time; our 'eyes are open' but 'their sense are shut'.

Can therapy but take notes from somnambulists? Of what use is personal, confessional, even therapeutic poetry, itself a form of celebrity autobiography, if we are asleep? What kind of poetry can awaken modern man from the strong satisfactions of memory? The 'Hell' that Lady Macbeth half-sees and dreams is 'murky': it is our world in the twenty-first century. Alarmingly, we might just be fulfilling the prophecies in *Macbeth* today: at the beginning, we see ourselves through the play's glass murkily, by the end, 'face to face' (1 Corinthians 13. 12).

Banquo challenges the witches after they have prophesied Macbeth's future: 'If you can looke into the Seedes of Time, | And say, which Graine will grow, and which will not, | Speake then to me' (I. iii. 58-60). It would seem that for Wordsworth a spot is a particle like a seed or a drop, and perhaps also a place. Spots of time are seeds of past experience that grow up inside an individual's life to nourish his imagination; they are memory places to which we may have recourse when we are depressed. The major point of Wordsworth's autobiographical poem is that

'Fair seed-time had my soul, and I grew up | Foster'd alike by beauty and by fear' (*1805 Prelude*, I. 306-7). But should the adult poet eat of the resulting kind of fructifying tree within? Is Wordsworth also saying darkly that there are in our existence blemishes of time? When he coined his expression, 'spots of time', was he thinking consciously or unconsciously of Lady Macbeth's guilty inability to forget her past as well as Banquo's fatal curiosity about his future?

Most of the spots of time that Wordsworth remembers from his own life in *The Prelude* are moments when his younger self felt guilty or scared. It may have been that his submerged intention in writing this autobiographical poem was to purge himself of memory in order to write philosophical poetry. But like many poets today he became consumed by his memories and by nature, revising *The Prelude* intermittently until he died, instead of beginning a new epic poem. A Sufi poet or a Neoplatonist philosopher would have chastised Wordsworth for dwelling so much on his own past. As a self-proclaimed poet-teacher he should have learned to look after, not before.

If we take the larger view of our existence and accept that there is life before and after death, as Wordsworth in fact does in his 'Ode on the Intimations of Immortality in Youth', then our entire world is a spot that defiles the immortal soul. Milton uses the very word spot to describe this earth at the beginning of his 'Mask', the elaborate courtly play first presented at Ludlow Castle in 1634, called *Comus*. 'The first Scene discovers a wilde Wood' and '*The attendant Spirit descends or enters*'. He describes Heaven where he lives in relation to our filthy earth:

Before the starry threshold of *Joves* Court
My mansion is, where those immortal shapes
Of bright aëreal Spirits live insphear'd
In Regions milde of calm and serene Ayr,
Above the smoak and stirr of this dim spot,

> Which men call Earth, and with low-thoughted care
> Confin'd, and pester'd in this pin-fold here,
> Strive to keep up a frail, and Feaverish being
> Unmindfull of the crown that Vertue gives
> After this mortal change, to her true Servants
> Amongst the enthron'd gods on Sainted seats. (*Comus*, 1-11)

That 'Which men call Earth', our smoky and busy world, this guardian spirit calls a 'dim spot'. In fact, he lives on the real surface of the Earth in a 'mansion', or dwelling-place, before Jove's Court. As Socrates points out in Plato's *Phaedo*,

> The earth itself is pure and lies in the pure sky where the stars are situated, which the majority of those who discourse on these subjects call the ether. The water and mist and air are the sediment of the ether and they always flow into the hollows of the earth. We, who dwell in the hollows of it, are unaware of this and we think that we live above, on the surface of the earth. (1997: 93; 109c)

It is very easy during our scientific age, on what we now know to be our round planet, in the wake of modern astronomy and space travel, to scoff at Socrates. But I believe that we betray a larger ignorance by dismissing his view of the earth. The scientific outlook is just a very refined way of living in a hollow of mist:

> living in a certain hollow of the earth, we believe that we live upon its surface; the air we call the heavens... because of our weakness and slowness we are not able to make our way to the upper limit of the air; if anyone got to this upper limit, if anyone came to it or reached it on wings and his head rose above it, then just as fish on rising from the sea see things in our region, he would see things there and, if his nature could endure to contemplate them, he would know that there is the

> true heaven, the true light and the true earth, for the earth here, these stones and the whole region, are spoiled and eaten away, just as things in the sea are by the salt water. (1997: 94; 109e-110a)

Where is this 'true heaven', this 'true earth'? Can we reach it merely by propelling our bodies upwards in a space shuttle? Socrates would not have believed in the efficacy of NASA or Richard Branson: we reach the upper limits, the 'true heaven', by other means than jet propulsion. We need another kind of 'wings'. As Lars von Triers sensibly replied on being asked whether we are alone in the universe: '"We are... But no one wants to realize it. They keep wanting to push limits and fly wherever,' he laughs. 'Forget it! Look inward'" (Thorsen 2011).

If we all exist within the mind of God, and we know that mind to be within us, then Socrates' archaic or quaint astronomy begins to make more sense. My syncretic mind races from the beginning of western philosophy to the end of the Bible: 'And I saw a new heaven, and a new earth: for the first heaven, and the first earth were passed away, and there was no more sea' (Revelation 21. 1); no more drifting upon a 'darkening flood' (Yeats 1950: 276). Poetry helps our nature to endure in 'the true light', to contemplate such things as are undiscoverable in space. It helps us to be fish out of our element.

A moment in each day

Milton's different uses of the word 'spot' and its variants in *Paradise Lost* darken still further Wordsworth's 'spots of time'. Satan's shield, tempered in celestial fire, but perhaps battered by his fall to Hell, is likened to the moon, a 'spotty Globe'. Milton had visited the '*Tuscan* Artist', Galileo, in 1638, perhaps seeing for himself the spots on the moon through his powerful telescope. The Italian astronomer had believed those spots to be 'new Lands, | Rivers or Mountains' (I. 284-91), but the sociable angel,

Raphael, will later contradict these theories, informing Adam that the moon's spots are, in fact, 'unpurg'd | Vapours not yet into her substance turnd' (V. 419-20). Such a view is supported by the Roman natural philosopher, Pliny the Elder, who says in his encyclopaedic *Natural History*, 'these spots be nothing else but the dregs of the earth, caught up with other moisture among the vapours' (Milton 1998: 307) since 'of Elements | The grosser feeds the purer' (V. 415-6). The moon's spots are gross matter, dregs or mists, not promising new lands, if we are to believe a supernatural being and an ancient writer, rather than an early modern scientist.

Even more ominously, when Satan lands on the sun, having escaped Hell to confound somehow God's new creation, man, he is:

a spot like which perhaps
Astronomer in the Sun's lucent Orbe
Through his glaz'd Optic Tube yet never saw. (III. 588-90)

Galileo's heavily tinted telescope allows him to discern sunspots, which we now know to be cavities in the photosphere filled with cooler vapours, but such an optic tube will not help him to see that altogether different kind of spot, Satan on the sun.

The word 'spot' becomes more portentous as the poem progresses. From the sun, Satan spots 'new Lands', the earth, which will become spotted in another sense by him. Before the fall, Adam and Eve live in 'spotless innocence' (IV. 318) in Paradise, and Adam reassures Eve after a bad dream (induced by Satan) that:

Evil into the mind of God or Man
May come and go, so unapprov'd, and leave
No spot or blame behind (V. 117-9)

– spot here meaning stigma or moral blemish. Christ's soul is 'unspotted' (V. 248), incapable of being corrupted by the grave or by Satan, which he acknowledges when he pledges to die to redeem man. But our world, 'this Earth' is 'a spot, a graine, | An Atom, with the Firmament compar'd': for Adam 'this opacous Earth', this dull place of mud, is 'this punctual spot' round which the heavenly bodies move, officiating light (VIII. 17-8 and 23).

The prophetic engraver-poet Blake would probably have accepted Wordsworth as the greatest poet of his age; he also understood his limitations as a thinker. With Milton in mind, he might have said that Wordsworth's work is too spotted: too full of unpurged dregs of earth. Such spots are satanic blemishes, although the soul will always remain spotless. Perhaps by dwelling on spots of time we can purge them from our existence, assimilate them to a new one. For Blake, Wordsworth dwells too much on this 'cloudy spot' (*Paradise Lost*, V. 266). Blake complains, 'I see in Wordsworth the Natural Man rising up against the Spiritual Man Continually & then he is No Poet but a Heathen Philosopher at Enmity against all true Poetry or Inspiration'. Wordsworth 'could wish my days to be | Bound each to each by natural piety'; Blake commented in the margin of his copy of this poem: 'There is no such Thing as Natural Piety Because The Natural Man is at Enmity with God' (2008: 665).

We can think of the difference between these two poets in terms of time. Rather than lie down and recall spots of time from our past like Wordsworth, Blake would make us alert to find eternity again each day. As we have already seen:

> There is a Moment in each Day that Satan cannot find
> Nor can his Watch Fiends find it, but the Industrious find
> This Moment & it multiply. & when it once is found
> It renovates every Moment of the Day if rightly placed[.]
> (*Milton*, Plate 35. 42-5)

Recalling that Satan for Blake is selfhood, we should understand that this moment in each day that escapes the everyday self contains Stevens' apprehension that 'God and the imagination are one' (1954: 524). Blake's lines come just when their speaker awakes to vision, having lost consciousness on his garden path, just when the skylark is rising to the morning odour of wild thyme, greeting the new day with his song. I would rather find industriously a moment out of time in each day than brood over spots of time in my childhood. This book asks you to become industrious in the manner of Blake and Stevens so that a moment in your reading of a poem can renovate every moment of your day.

Why am I being so hard on Wordsworth? In fact, I am judging him by his, or Coleridge's, early standards to try and understand our contradictory selves in the modern world.

In 1800, newly established in the Lake District after returning from Germany and a youth of wandering, Wordsworth says effectively, 'bring it on':

> *Come thou prophetic Spirit, that inspir'st*
> *The human Soul of universal earth,*
> *Dreaming on things to come; and dost possess*
> *A metropolitan Temple in the hearts*
> *Of mighty Poets; upon me bestow*
> *A gift of genuine insight; that my Song*
> *With star-like virtue in its place may shine;*
> *Shedding benignant influence, – and secure,*
> *Itself, from all malevolent effect*
> *Of those mutations that extend their sway*
> *Throughout the nether sphere!* (2009: 2. 302-3)

These lines were used 'as a kind of *Prospectus* of the design and scope' (2009: 2. 300) of the philosophical epic *The Recluse*, which Wordsworth was unable to complete, and for which *The Prelude* serves as an autobiographical prelude. Although his verse certainly does console many today, it does not live 'as a Light hung up in heaven' (2009: 1. 586) as he hoped. Instead

Wordsworth's '*Song*' is of this dim spot the earth because he did not manage to '*secure*' his poetry '*from all malevolent effect*', and we discover its supernatural greatnesses between the lines.

Was it for this?

Wordsworth came to write the poem that was eventually published as *The Prelude* almost by chance. In the winter of 1798 and 1799, the coldest of the eighteenth century, he was isolated with his sister Dorothy in Goslar on the edge of the Harz Forest in Germany:

> With the protection of a [green] pelisse lined with [fox] fur, & a [black] dog's-skin bonnet, such as was worn by the peasants, I walked daily on the ramparts, or in a sort of public ground or garden, in which was a pond. Here I had no companion but a Kings fisher, a beautiful creature that used to glance by me. I consequently became much attached to it. (2007: 113)

Returning from one of those walks in October, Wordsworth picked up a small notebook bound in boards, which Dorothy had been using to write an account of their journey from Hamburg to Goslar, while making notes on German grammar, and in which he had written part of a moral essay. Starting at the back of that book and working backwards, 'mostly by pairs of pages in a zigzag fashion', 'writing across or along the page as the fancy took him', as his modern editors note, Wordsworth unwittingly began writing what would become his major work. I like to think that he was still wearing his dog's-skin bonnet, consumed by this sudden effusion of poetry. But he had probably taken it off because, as Dorothy records, their rooms were stoved: their 'summer warmth makes a contrast with the external air, that sets the flesh a creeping, even when you go through the passages and staircases' (de Selincourt 1967: 245).

The notebook that contains this exciting manuscript still

exists: its importance was first recognized in the 1930s and it is now in the Wordsworth Library at Grasmere. It has been photographed as part of *The Cornell Wordsworth*, a series of books that deals with all versions of Wordsworth's poems from drafting stages to final printings. Modern scholarship has proven that Wordsworth was embarked upon a poem to rival *Paradise Lost*, not bothering with an initial capital letter, beginning, in fact, half-way through a line.

Seven years later, this short draft of October 1798, now known as Manuscript JJ, had been transformed into a thirteen-book epic 'Poem (title not yet fixed upon) to Coleridge'. But it was only published, after many revisions and in fourteen books, just after Wordsworth's death in 1850, with the following lines revised a little and embedded some way into Book I:

was it for this
That one, the fairest of all rivers,
loved
To blend his murmurs with my nurse's song
And from his alder shades and rocky falls
t
And from his fords and shallows send}
a voice
To intertwine my dreams[.] (1977: 115)

This original opening of *The Prelude* is transcribed here verbatim from the 1798 notebook: the symbol } connotes an overwriting.

When Wordsworth incorporates these lines into the longer versions of the poem, he makes the antecedent of the 'this' in the first line, his writer's block in Goslar. He has been unable to write another kind of philosophical poem, which he had planned with Coleridge to be his life's work, and which was to be called, as we have seen, *The Recluse*:

some philosophic Song
Of Truth that cherishes our daily life;
With meditations passionate from deep
Recesses in man's heart, immortal verse
Thoughtfully fitted to the Orphean lyre[.]

Since he cannot write this kind of poem Wordsworth seeks:

repose
In indolence from vain perplexity,
Unprofitably travelling towards the grave,
Like a false Steward who hath much receiv'd
And renders nothing back. (*1805 Prelude,* I. 231-5 and 268-72)

He is wasting, by not using, his poetic talent for its intended purposes. His reposeful indolence seems unindustrious. In the notes to his various student editions of *The Prelude,* Jonathan Wordsworth argues that Wordsworth is turning to his childhood to work out what impedes him, inadvertently beginning one poem to find out why he cannot begin the one he should. 'Almost at once, however, it must have been apparent to him that as well as stimulating reproaches, his childhood memories could provide material that would actually replace the philosophy that Coleridge expected him to produce' (Wordsworth 1979b: 572).

Another scholar, Stephen Parrish, looking closely at the notebook in which Wordsworth first began his poem, sees that there are drafts of lines that may precede the 'was it for this' passage. Wordsworth wrote 'was it for this' on the penultimate page of the notebook; the following lines are on the very last page, which would have been Wordsworth's first page since he was working backwards through the book:

inspiration
a mild creative breeze

a gentle inspiration
a vital breeze that passes gently on
the[?]
Oer things which it has made and
soon becomes
A tempest a redundant energy
That sweeps the waters and the [?mountain] [?power]
Creating not but as it may
disturbing things created. –

a storm not terrible but
strong
with lights and shades and with
a rushing power
with loveliness and power

trances of thought
And mountings of the mind compared
to which
The wind that drives along th autumnal
lefa
Is meekness. (1977: 117)

Wordsworth was probably writing very quickly and these lines are very rough: what may be revisions are shown in italics just above the lines to which they pertain; '*[?mountain] [?power]*' are conjectural readings; for 'lefa' we should probably read 'leaf'. But some of this scrawl does come to constitute the opening lines or 'Glad Preamble' of *The Prelude* in its longer states of 1805-6 and 1850.

Parrish argues that this page of fragmentary verse provides 'the only clue we have to the original antecedent of "was it for this"'. The 'this' is not a simple case of writer's block, an inability to write 'some philosophic Song': '"This" seems here to have been the powerful disturbance of mind occasioned by a superabundant flow of inspiration – not incapacity, or guilt, or self-reproach' that Wordsworth describes in later versions of *The Prelude*. 'The tone of "was it for this" may not, in fact, be ironic, or regretful, but wondering, perhaps confused, even perhaps quietly exultant' (Wordsworth 1977: 6). The 'this' Wordsworth refers to is 'a mild creative breeze' that soon becomes 'A tempest a redundant energy': he feels gather within 'a storm not terrible but strong | with lights and shades and with a rushing power'. For Wordsworth the word 'redundant' may have retained something of the force of its Latin etymon, *redundans*, meaning overflowing or abounding.

No one should deny the power and importance of the poem that emerges out of this mood and Wordsworth's half-guilty revelation that creative attention to childhood memories could replace the labour of making a philosophical epic poem. According to Wordsworth himself, he was 'obliged to write in self-defence', enduring the wintry isolation of Goslar without books, although the very act of writing provoked 'uneasiness at my stomach and side, with a dull pain about my heart' (de Selincourt 1967: 236). *The Prelude* is always more than an account of the poet's childhood and youth; 'it is also implicitly', as Stephen Gill notes, a sensitive 'record of Wordsworth's intellectual journey between 1799 and 1805' (Wordsworth 2000: xxiii). The greatness of the poetry lies in what Jonathan Wordsworth calls its 'double awareness': we respond to Wordsworth's spots of time '*both as child and as adult*' (Wordsworth 1979b: 576).

The spots of time that Wordsworth remembers in this very first draft of *The Prelude* describe, as does Plato's *Phaedo*, 'numerous hollows of many kinds and shapes and sizes into which the water and the mist and the air have gathered' (1997: 94; 109b). Wordsworth recalls his earliest memories as if he has newly descended from the ether into one of its hollows as a stream tumbles down from the mountains: when he did 'love |

To range through half the night among the cliffs | And the smooth hollows'. Even when roving 'In the high places, on the lonely peaks' the young Wordsworth is still 'Among the mountains & the winds' in valleys that catch the sediment of the ether (1977: 105 and 113).On the edge of such a hollow, sustained by smaller hollows, we find him bird's-nesting:

Oh when I have hung
Above the ravens nest, have hung alone
By half inch fissures in the slippery rock
But ill sustained and almost as it seemed
Suspended by the wind which blew amain
Against the naked cragg ah then
While on the perilous edge I hung alone
With what strange utterance did the loud dry wind
Blow through my ears the sky seemed not a sky
Of earth, and with what motion moved the clouds[.] (1977: 124)

Wordsworth may have been roped and let down by other boys from the edge of the cliff; in later versions, before the boy is hung alone, 'Roved we', in the plural, 'as plunderers where the Mother-bird | Had in high places built her lodge' (*1850 Prelude*, I. 327-8). Ravens were a threat to lambs on the Cumbrian hills and the parish would have offered a reward for the nest.

The passage itself hangs 'on the perilous edge'. Reading across and down from 'Oh when' to 'ah then' we are roped by Wordsworth's lines that describe the boy's hanging down as Constable's or Turner's textured brushstrokes might: the poet's lines of sound intensify even a Romantic painter's strokes of paint since we hear as well as see them, and the medium of language impels us forwards in time by describing a scene from the past.

Hung down by a line and a half of *v* sounds, 'when I have hung | Above the raven's nest', hooped by the repetition of 'have hung', readers find themselves 'By half-inch fissures in the slippery rock | But ill-sustained': vertical steps are taken across the lines, slippery *s* sounds finding temporary footholds in *st* sounds, 'and almost, as it seemed, | Suspended by the wind which blew amain | Against the naked cragg'; the windy *w* sounds blow 'amain | Agains*t*' the foot of their next line, poet and boy in treacherous step as they move down the naked crag with metrical and physical feet. Describing the boy's taking of tentative non-steps against rock and on air, the poet makes confident steps for the eye and ear in 'the language of the sense' (Wordsworth 2009: 1. 375); my reading partakes of both: we respond as child and as adult.

Where does that leave us? Now that we have been hung down with assurance by the length of five lines of periphrasis what are we to notice? Now that we too hang 'on the perilous edge' of a hollow with the boy and the remembering poet, 'With what strange utterance did the loud dry wind | Blow through my ears'. As John Caputo asks of 'the old word *per-sona, personare,* the person as sounding through, resonating' and of the voice that sounds through the face of suffering:

> What is stirring in these words? Whose voice speaks? What is the more than human 'It' (*das 'Es'*) which speaks whenever man speaks, which makes itself heard, if we are attentive enough, whenever human words are uttered? What abyss breaks through here? What is playing itself out here? (1987: 290)

Jonathan Wordsworth argues that 'It is finally the vision of the child that we are left with, because the child as borderer is the guarantee of his creator's adult strength.' He sees Wordsworth as preoccupied with border-states, between this world and the other realm. 'Though no transcendental claims are being made, the force of the poetry persuades one to read the final line more as a question than an exclamation' (1984: 41-2): 'the sky seemed not a sky | Of earth, and with what motion moved the clouds!' With what resonates boy and poem? How do we address 'the force of the poetry' that 'persuades' despite its poet's more sophisticated intentions?

Wordsworth's poetry is great here because it contains a poignant tension between wondering child and rational adult. It is nonetheless sad because the mature poet's gently mocking scepticism really just makes him into a somnambulist slipping into 'the smoak and stirr of this dim spot'. I would argue that his younger self, despite the older poet's assured conjuring of that boy almost as vision, is of no help ultimately. It is no guarantee of future creativity unless Wordsworth is content merely to write about his personal history. The poet must know himself from the future in eternity rather than enumerate spots of time from his past. Memory will never be an adequate substitute for perennial wisdom.

I understand that the sea to which 'one, the fairest of all rivers', travels is also the sea of time and space. Wordsworth's superabundance of inspiration, which causes him to open a notebook at its end and begin writing shards of verse, is 'a storm not terrible but strong | with lights and shades and with a rushing power'. But it does not, in fact, uplift the poet with 'mountings of the mind' when he turns the page of that notebook to write 'was it for this'. Because Wordsworth chooses to remember his childhood on this 'dim spot', his mind, instead of mounting in its trances, is doomed, like Yeats's swan, emblem of man's soul in 'Coole and Ballylee, 1931', to drift downstream, passively at twilight, on the confusion of our materialist age.

Earlier in 'Coole and Ballylee, 1931', the speaker is surprised by the sound of 'the mounting swan' and he turns to see the rushing power of it becoming 'That stormy white' in the sky, his description acknowledging that it is also an emblem of the wondering and exultant 'mood' of the inspired soul. It is almost as if Yeats has created a fresh poem out of Wordsworth's rough lines about 'A tempest... | That sweeps the waters' on the last page of his notebook:

At sudden thunder of the mounting swan
I turned about and looked where branches break
The glittering reaches of the flooded lake.

Another emblem there! That stormy white
But seems a concentration of the sky;
And, like the soul, it sails into the sight
And in the morning's gone, no man knows why;
And is so lovely that it sets to right
What knowledge or its lack had set awry,
So arrogantly pure, a child might think
It can be murdered with a spot of ink. (1950: 275-6)

Wordsworth may well be murdering 'the mounting swan' – 'a rushing power' of 'mountings of the mind'; by recording in ink, spots of time from his childhood, his poem retards the soul that he must make.

As ever I cannot help but think of *Macbeth*: the protagonist's first mention of 'murder' takes on uncanny resonance if one imagines the following lines spoken by Wordsworth in the cold October of 1798:

Present Feares
Are lesse then horrible Imaginings:
My thought, whose Murther yet is but fantasticall,
Shakes so my single state of Man,
That Function is smother'd in surmise,
And nothing is, but what is not. (I. iii. 137-42)

Wordsworth's thought is not of murder but his mood as he begins *The Prelude* is murderous in its own way. His inspiration, 'a mild creative breeze', soon becomes 'A tempest a redundant energy', 'Creating not but as it may | disturbing things created': as Macbeth sees, 'This supernaturall soliciting | Cannot be ill; cannot be good' (I. iii. 130-1). More alarmingly, Wordsworth may well be murdering thought. Wordsworth's 'single state of Man', his unified body and soul, has been shaken by intimations that such a state is horribly paradoxical if one acknowledges the soul to be eternal. But, by then writing autobiographical verse, he is treading dangerously close to what Blake called 'Single vision & Newtons sleep', a Macbethian materialism that keeps us from a 'fourfold vision' of our real situation on this dim spot (2008: 722). It is comforting to remember one's childhood after divine explosions within but the immortal soul requires a different kind of poetry than autobiography.

Both Macbeth and Wordsworth are unsettled because each soul is brought to crisis by what Yeats would call 'personifying spirits' (1980: 272) who care little for the everyday circumstances of our lives. The 'horrid Image' that the witches conjure in Macbeth's imagination makes his 'seated Heart knock at my Ribbes' (I. iii. 135-6). Wordsworth too is queasy 'with a dull pain about my heart. I have used the word pain, but uneasiness and heat are words which more accurately express my feeling' (de Selincourt 1967: 236). Both find 'That Function is smother'd in surmise'. For Macbeth 'surmise' is unwarranted conjecture, hence imagination, which smothers the right action of a sane man, causing him to act madly or not at all. Wordsworth's poetic function is at once suffocated and inspired by supernatural powers within his imagination.

On the last page of that notebook shared with Dorothy in the winter of 1798-99 Wordsworth half-intimates that 'God and the imagination are one...' But when he turns the page and asks 'was it for this' he looks for signs of that supernatural presence in the wrong direction. As Yeats well knew, 'The soul cannot have much knowledge till it has shaken off the habit of time and of place'

(1959: 358); Wordsworth mistakenly has recourse to these spots. Like Macbeth his response to something greater than he knows is worldly and ultimately tragic: *The Prelude* will not enable Wordsworth to complete that which he sees as his life's work, the projected philosophical epic poem, *The Recluse*.

I do not believe that Yeats intended the uncanny correspondence between his 'Coole and Ballylee, 1931', in which the speaker turns to see the swan taking off from the lake and then imagines it dying on a river, and the two openings of Wordsworth's *Prelude*. But Yeats's emblematic poem teaches me indirectly that Wordsworth had surrendered to our phase of history, by substituting memory in the place of philosophy, letting confusion fall upon his thought: 'And nothing is, but what is not'.

Wordsworth's spots of time are of this dim earth; Yeats's mounting swan is a concentration of the sky that is so arrogantly pure it is dangerously evanescent, unassailable by spots of words. His subsequent vision of its death downstream is a chilling description of our ignorant age. Wordsworth's river, even though it is described in fairy-tale-ish fashion as 'the fairest of all rivers', is more realistic than symbolic and Yeats would have seen that as half of Wordsworth's problem: he should have been swimming secretly against our current realism like a salmon, the living symbol of knowledge in the Old Norse Scriptures.

Lines added to his first draft of *The Prelude* when Wordsworth came to copy them out prove that the poet knew in his heart that he was travelling in the wrong direction. Addressing perhaps Dorothy, or more likely Coleridge, Wordsworth explains that in this present unplanned poem he is listening to:

> Reproaches from my former years, whose power
> May spur me on, in mankind now mature,
> To honourable toil. (*1799 Prelude*, I. 451-3)

The poet is pre-empting criticism from close friends who are expecting him to write poetry that looks in the opposite direction to the poem that he is now transcribing. As Parrish says, 'here for the first time are signs on the speaker's part of a concern to justify the self-indulgence of composing these boyhood memories'; this new ending, a result of Wordsworth's anxious revisions after transcription, 'introduces a distinctly darker tone' (1977: 13):

> Yet, should it be
> That this is but an impotent desire,
> That I by such enquiry am not taught
> To understand myself, nor thou to know
> With better knowledge how the heart was framed
> Of him thou lovest, need I dread from thee
> Harsh judgements if I am so loth to quit
> Those recollected hours that have the charm
> Of visionary things, and lovely forms
> And sweet sensations that throw back our life
> And make our infancy a visible scene
> On which the sun is shining? – (*1799 Prelude*, I. 453-64)

Wordsworth is most concerned to make his new poem at least sunny-sounding. But we should recall that Macbeth's 'Castle hath a pleasant seat, | The ayre nimbly and sweetly recommends it selfe | Unto our gentle sences'. Wordsworth would like Coleridge to say of his burgeoning poem what the doomed Banquo says of his murderous friend's abysmal home: 'that the Heavens breath | Smells wooingly here' (I. vi. 1-3 and 5-6). Despite its indisputable allurement, and Wordsworth is charmed to make it into, finally, fourteen books, the poem that becomes *The Prelude* nonetheless dooms its poet to fall into Lady Macbeth's kind of somnambulism.

Others have been likewise wooed and different kinds of doctors have been taking notes. Therapeutic autobiography now pervades literature and psychology. Memory lures patients and writers to self-indulgence, if not quite always to 'the wordsworthian or egotistical sublime' (Keats 2002: 147). Notes are taken only 'to satisfie [our] remembrance the more strongly'. Academics have been busy producing scrupulous and expensive editions of the poet's rough drafts. But Milton's attendant spirit in *Comus* would say that Wordsworth, even like Macbeth himself, is on the road to being 'Unmindfull of the crown that Vertue gives | After this mortal change'.

By such enquiry as *The Prelude* the poet is not taught to understand himself. What is the philosophy or perennial wisdom that Wordsworth was evading by turning to his childhood memories? It is that of civilizations before our Renaissance, but it is also to be found in Spenser, Shakespeare, Milton, Blake, and Yeats, poets who all believed in the omnipotence of truth that comes to us from the future: whether they knew it or not, their poems are, as Yeats asserted, 'Proof that there's a purpose set | Before the secret working mind: | Profane perfection of mankind' (1950: 399).

Gentle powers

Wordsworth's first draft of *The Prelude* contains another spot of time in which we find beings not only of the earth's hollows. Still addressing his uneasy mood of redundant inspiration during a freezing German winter, the poet asks:

> For this, when on the witherd mountain slope
> The frost and breath of frosty wind had nippd
> The last autumnal crocus did I love
> To range through half the night among the cliffs
> And the smooth hollows where the woodcocks ran
> Along the moonlight turf. In thought and wish
> That time my shoulder all with springes hung
> I was a fell destroyer[.] (1977: 125-6)

Are spots of time, in fact, misty hollows in our true existence? Have our modern preoccupations with autobiography, scientific discourse, technology and space travel been hung around us like the traps or 'springes' that the young Wordsworth shoulders as 'a fell destroyer', the hero of his own mock epic, among 'the smooth hollows'?

Wordsworth's 'springes' are carried to catch woodcocks, which is at once literally true and recalls Polonius' proverbial description of Hamlet's vows: the woodcock was supposed easily caught and the callow Ophelia has fallen for Hamlet's charms or 'Springes to catch Woodcocks' (*Hamlet*, I. iii. 115). Blake saw that the 'nets & gins & traps' that we carry are 'cold floods of abstraction' (*Visions of the Daughters of Albion*, Plate 5, 18-20). Prevalent empiricist reasoning is based on our experience of the dark waters of time and space; it is designed to ensnare that matter but it also traps us. We have been easily caught by our own mechanisms. We think that we can explore further than ever before. We wonder at space travel and delight in taking cheap international flights. From the viewpoint of another dimension, which we reasonably deny, we appear to be ignorant provincials.

As Wordsworth continues with this spot of time he addresses supernatural powers:

Gentle power[s],
Who give us happiness & call it peace
When running on from snare to snare I plied
My anxious visitation hurrying on
Still hurryin[g] onward, how my heart
Panted: among the lonely eughtrees & the crags
That looked upon me how my bosom beat
With hope & fear. – Sometimes strong desire
Resistless over came me & the bird
Th[at] was the captive of another's toils
Became my prey, and then [ ] I heard

> Low breathings coming after me and sounds
> Of undistinguishable motion steps
> Almost as silent as the turf they trod. (1977: 126)

A sceptical reading of this passage sees that the boy's guilt at having stolen a bird, trapped by another poacher, makes him paranoid. The adult poet understands that the boy's sense of being followed was a delusion: the 'Low breathings' and 'sounds | Of undistinguishable motion', the spooky 'steps | Almost as silent as the turf they trod', are all in the boy's head. Why, then, does the poet address these lines to gentle powers? Wordsworth may have found it difficult to answer that question himself but I feel that modern readers can be too quick to dismiss such apostrophizing.

Just what are these gentle powers? Three years before Wordsworth composed these lines, Anna Laetitia Barbauld had reissued Mark Akenside's poem, *The Pleasures of Imagination,* which Coleridge was fond of quoting, if not always referencing. Like Wordsworth in *The Prelude,* Akenside would unfold in his verse 'With what attractive charms this goodly frame | Of nature touches the consenting hearts | Of mortal men' and poets, and he thus commands the genii of poetry:

> Attend, ye gentle powers
> Of musical delight! and while I sing
> Your gifts, your honours, dance around my strain. (Akenside 2000: 11)

Wordsworth's gentle powers are related to Akenside's, but I do not believe that Wordsworth is only making an allusion to *The Pleasures of Imagination* at the beginning of *The Prelude.* In different ways, both Wordsworth and Akenside believed in fairies, although neither may have admitted such superstitious faith, even to themselves.

The first draft of *The Prelude* is too full of supernatural beings to expel them quickly to a neoclassical spirit world. There are two apostrophes to guardian spirits among the spots of time, when Wordsworth addresses 'ye beings of the hills' and 'ye spirits of the springs | And ye that have your voices in the clouds | And ye that are familiars of the Lakes | And standing pools' (1977: 125). I will return to these gentle beings in the next chapter, to find them also in Shakespeare and Ovid, because I do not 'read past them easily enough' as did my dear old late tutor Jonathan Wordsworth (see 1979b: 573).

I believe in Wordsworth's supernatural and gentle beings. Many scholars today claim that they were intended merely as an imitation of such creatures as Alexander Pope's sylphs in *The Rape of the Lock*; strangely their new home in Wordsworth's lines has made them effectual again. As in Shakespeare and Milton, Wordsworth's spirits are prompt beings, of use also in folklore, which have been summoned into the poetry. If the call may have been playful and urbane, and hence almost inadvertent, it was answered nonetheless. Banished from nature by modern sceptical habits of mind these gentle beings have found a new mansion or dwelling-place in some of our poems. While we have been busy trying to catch other matter in cold floods of abstraction, unwittingly entrapping ourselves with scientific materialism in the process, these helpful spirits slipped into our literature.

In early drafts of *Comus*, Milton's '*attendant Spirit*' is 'A Guardian spirit, or Dæmon' (1972: 13). Readers today only tolerate his presence in the 'Mask' by diminishing him to a neoclassical ornament. I accept him at face value as an intermediary between Heaven and earth. He is an odd compound creature who lives 'Before the starry threshold of *Joves* Court' but who also seems unconventionally Christian, making allusions to the New Testament when he explains that he helps those who aspire to enter 'the Palace of Eternity':

> Yet som there be that by due steps aspire
> To lay there just hands on that Golden Key
> That ope's the Palace of Eternity:
> To such my errand is, and but for such,
> I would not soil these pure Ambrosial weeds,
> With the rank vapours of this Sin-worn mould. (*Comus*, 12-17)

This guardian spirit is willing to soil his immortal clothes with the foul-smelling air of this earth to help some to lay their hands on 'that Golden Key'. Jesus said to Peter when he gave him the keys to the Kingdom of Heaven: 'and whatsoever thou shalt bind on earth, shall be bound in heaven: whatsoever thou shalt loose on earth, shall be loosed in heaven' (Matthew 16. 19). The first edition of the King James Bible directs us from this passage to John 20. 23. On the evening of the day of his Resurrection Jesus reveals himself to his disciples:

> Then said Jesus to them againe, Peace be unto you: As my father hath sent me, even so I send you. And when he had said this, hee breathed on them, and saith unto them, Receive ye the holy Ghost. Whose soever sinnes yee remit, they are remitted unto them, and whose soever sinnes yee retaine, they are retained. (John 20. 21-3)

It is significant that in *Comus*, we are each capable of receiving 'that Golden Key'. Milton's guardian spirit has taken the key from Peter and would help each of us who is in earnest to lay our hands on it, in the same way that Jesus breathed 'the holy Ghost' into each of his disciples in The Gospel according to John. Poetry also is a gift of the 'holy Ghost'; it contains 'a mild creative breeze' that opens the Kingdom of Heaven within.

Blake changes 'that Golden Key' to 'the end of a golden string' in his apostrophe to the Christians in *Jerusalem*:

I give you the end of a golden string,
Only wind it into a ball:
It will lead you in at Heavens gate,
Built in Jerusalems wall. (Plate 77)

For the poet-prophet, Christian Revelation is incomplete. As Jung said, 'God, in the shape of the Holy Ghost, puts up his tent in man, for he is obviously minded to realize himself continually not only in Adam's descendants, but in an indefinitely large number of believers, and possibly in mankind as a whole' (1984: 84). As Yeats succinctly puts it, 'Love has pitched his mansion in | The place of excrement' (1950: 295). Orthodox Christian doctrine, since the time of Aquinas, practices and encourages the worship of the Son at the expense of the Holy Spirit within the soul. No wonder since the Holy Spirit eludes all control of the Church, which must always be organized.

Blake might have noticed that Christ's words to Peter echo a mantra of alchemy: 'as above, so below' (Raine 2002: 49). Poetry contains such a key to an apprehension of the immortality of the soul. But it need not concern itself with such institutional organization as the Church, which Peter represents, since he is held to be the first of the popes. Poetry can accept the Holy Spirit and unruly guardian spirits serving this 'bounteous power' (1977: 126), which Wordsworth also addresses and glosses as 'inspiration... a gentle inspiration' in the first draft of *The Prelude*. Poems of this power have taken the keys to the Palace of Eternity from Peter and his Church.

I expect that you still regard Milton's guardian spirit as a quaint piece of Renaissance decoration, another neoclassical device. Most modern editions of Wordsworth's *Prelude* will tell you with great assurance that his 'gentle beings' come from this literary tradition. I believe in their usefulness: such spirits have descended and entered spots of poetry, and those who by due steps aspire to lay their hands on 'that Golden Key' must learn to consult carefully with them. Such an attitude seems laughably provincial and old-fashioned today. I would probably risk ridicule or worse if I were to express these beliefs at an academic conference.

Surely, modern common-sense complains, we know better than to be so superstitious. I reply that all of the great poets, from Homer to Yeats, would have believed in such powers during their most intense moments of creativity. In fact, these spirits may well be just as bemused at our modern ignorance of them when we sit trapped on international flights, or in seminars at conferences, exploring physically or theoretically our limited realm, the flood of time and space. Luckily these gentle powers flocked to literature during the times when their oral traditions were dying out in the late sixteenth century in England and in the late nineteenth century in Ireland. Even so their case may well be more serious than we think since they depend on us just as much as we think we can do without them.

John Carey's note to the attendant Spirit's prologue in his edition of Milton uses Plutarch's *Moralia* to emphasize the beneficence of 'daemons':

> they are the souls of those who have 'done with the contests of life, and by prowess of soul become daemons': they aid those souls on earth which strive towards virtue: they live on the moon, just outside the earth's shadow: theirs is an intermediary state – they await the separation of soul and mind, when mind will finally return to the sun – this is why Milton's daemon dwells *before* the threshold of Jove's court: they can descend from the moon to the earth 'as warders against misdeeds and chastisers of them': the earth below appears to them as an 'abyss' from which are heard 'innumerable roars and groans of animals, the wailing of innumerable babes, the mingled lamentations of men and women'. (Milton 2007a: 179)

Yeats acknowledges with more chilling insight that the aim of such guardian spirits, which he calls 'Gate-keepers' or 'personifying spirits' (1980: 272), is to make us persons that can be sounded through with the 'strange utterance' of suffering: 'through their dramatic power they bring our souls to crisis [...] They have but one purpose, to bring their chosen man to the greatest obstacle he may confront without despair'. We should also be aware that, like the spirits who helped Yeats write *A Vision*, supernatural beings can mislead as well as guide. We have to be wary of finding ourselves 'astray upon the Path of the Chameleon, upon Hodos Chameliontos' (Yeats 1980: 272 and 270).

Chapter 2

Ye Elves

Supernatural aid

We should be careful to distinguish the attendant or guardian spirit at the beginning of Milton's *Comus* from the flock of spiritual beings that haunt the first draft of Wordsworth's *Prelude*. In fact there exist various elaborate taxonomies of fairies, which can accommodate these particular supernatural powers. Agrippa knew, 'Many and divers are the names of good spirits, and bad', although he also cautioned: 'their proper, and true names, as those of the stars, are known to God alone' (2004: 532). Charles Upton would probably agree that Wordsworth's spirits embody – if that is the right word – 'the superhuman glamour with which the Regime of Nature can sometimes clothe the lyric poet – before the credit card bill comes due, that is' (2008: 131). Certainly we can say that the attendant spirit of *Comus* and the familiars of *The Prelude* are all tutelary spirits, but Wordsworth's powers seem more flagrantly pagan, literary and earthy than Milton's covertly Christian, Neoplatonic and heavenly creature.

Wordsworth, like Thomas the Rhymer in the ballad, 'was inspired by those forces of the intermediary plane or psychic realm known to the Greeks as the Muses and to the Arabs as the *jinn*, a word related to the Latin *genii*' (Upton 2008: 130). Today we might say that Wordsworth was a genius; he is admitting, in early drafts of *The Prelude*, that he had a *genius* or *genii*: his Muse was Nature and her host of familiar spirits. Milton's guardian spirit sounds more like a soul who is done with metempsychosis and the cycles of death and birth to which this material world is bound; he is a heavenly attendant, waiting on aspirant humans, while waiting for well-earned angelhood, before eternity in the future.

When poets deal with such beings as Wordsworth's 'familiars', care should be exercised; they risk becoming '"fay," a word meaning "fated," or "dedicated to a particular god"'. We should heed Upton's warning:

> Of course it is true that no-one who has not encountered and willingly placed himself under the power of his or her archetype, or genius, or tutelary deity can lead a fully human life. But there is also a way in which one's relationship to his or her tutelary deity, especially if it is unconscious, can diminish that humanity. (2008: 131)

Wordsworth's very first draft notes for his autobiographical poem, on the final page of Dorothy's German notebook, end with the half-line 'familiars of the lakes & stand[?ing]' (1977: 117); it is difficult to make out that last word in the manuscript because of an ink spot. When he came to shape these early scribblings of verse and notes into what we now call the *1799 Prelude*, such supernatural forms proliferate within the poem (later revisions made to these passages, when Wordsworth expanded *The Prelude* into a five-, a thirteen- and then a fourteen-book poem over the years, diminish, perhaps wisely, their presence).

As early as line 35 of the first fair copy of that poem, Wordsworth addresses 'Gentle Powers! | Who give us happiness and call it peace' (*1799 Prelude*, I. 35-6). By line 67, he elaborates on his belief in such beings:

> The mind of man is fashioned and built up
> Even as a strain of music: I believe
> That there are spirits, which, when they would form
> A favoured being, from his very dawn
> Of infancy do open out the clouds
> As at the touch of lightning, seeking him
> With gentle visitation; quiet Powers!

> Retired and seldom recognized, yet kind,
> And to the very meanest not unknown;
> With me, though rarely, [in my early days]
> They communed: others too there are who use,
> Yet happily aiming at the self-same end,
> Severer interventions, ministry
> More palpable, and of their school was I. (*1799 Prelude*, I. 67-80)

That Wordsworth should take the trouble to classify *genii* proves perhaps his stated belief in such spirits. The first order that he describes, made up of 'quiet Powers' that 'do open out the clouds | As at the touch of lightning', sounds like it could just about include the attendant spirit in *Comus*. The second kind, Wordsworth's guardians, are less reluctant to soil their 'pure Ambrosial weeds', perhaps do not even wear such heavenly garments, and are formed instead out of that which despoils such clothes: fashioned from 'the rank vapours of this Sin-worn mould', they use 'ministry | More palpable'.

Wordsworth's use of the word 'ministry' here recalls the opening of Coleridge's 'Frost at Midnight' where 'The frost performs its secret ministry, | Unhelped by any wind' (2001: 1. 453). Although '*Jack* frost performs *his* secret ministry, | Unhelped by any wind' sounds horribly sentimental, proto-Victorian even, Coleridge's personified frost that administers its office, dancing attendance outside while playing the role of minister to execute its spiritual work, does indeed recall that sprite. Certainly Coleridge was interested in local folklore, apparently lamenting to the young William Hazlitt in 1798 that:

> Wordsworth was not prone enough to believe in the traditional superstitions of the place and that there was something corporeal, a-matter-of-fact-ness, a clinging to the palpable, or often to the petty, in his poetry, in consequence. His genius was not a spirit that descended to him through the air; it

> sprung out of the ground like a flower, or unfolded itself from a green spray, on which the goldfinch sang. (Hazlitt 1982: 58)

Still very much under the influence of Coleridge and his superstitious beliefs when he came to write the first version of *The Prelude* in 1799, Wordsworth also sees that forms of this second species of the genus *genius* 'guided' him as a child: 'one evening, led by them, | I went alone to a Shepherd's boat, | ... | – She was an elfin pinnace' (*1799 Prelude*: I. 81-2 and 103).

Conversations with Coleridge during 1798 had probably made Wordsworth, at least temporarily, more prone to believe in traditional superstitions as an adult, as he had believed in pagan spirits during his boyhood. I would argue that such faith reignited makes him into an inviting power, despite himself, as he drafts rapidly his new poem. All sorts of supernatural beings swarm the first lines of the first draft of *The Prelude* to make their new abode there.

Modern critics like Kenneth Johnston have noted a seeming contrast between the 'intensely emotional concrete descriptions' of the 'spots of time' and the 'highly rhetorical abstract interpretations' (Hartman 1972: 5), assuming that these apostrophes to spiritual beings were added later like the supernatural machinery of Pope's *The Rape of the Lock*. But, as Jonathan Wordsworth points out, 'It isn't so. The personal experiences and abstract interpretations typically belong to the same moment' (1984: 421). The 'spots of time' are each made of the boy's credulity, his supposed intimations of supernatural forces at play when he feels scared (see *1799 Prelude*, I. 288-96); these spots are also divided from each other in the poem by the poet's invocations unto such supernatural guides, apostrophes that come notwithstanding the adult's natural or Wordsworthian scepticism about such matters:

> Ah! not in vain ye Beings of the hills!
> And ye that walk the woods and open heaths

By moon or star-light, thus from my first dawn
Of childhood did ye love to intertwine
The passions that build up our human soul,
Not with the mean and vulgar works of man,
But with high objects, with eternal things,
With life and nature, purifying thus
The elements of feeling and of thought,
And sanctifying by such discipline
Both pain and fear, until we recognise
A grandeur in the beatings of the heart. (*1799 Prelude*, I. 130-41)

Jonathan Wordsworth has argued that Wordsworth's 'belief in the One Life – a belief inspired by the Unitarian Coleridge' – so evident in the 'pantheism' of the 1798 poem 'Tintern Abbey', had, by 1799, 'been reduced to a literary, sub-classical spiritual world – "polytheism" might be the better word' (Wordsworth 1979b: 573). Although this critic does ask whether Wordsworth would have made a distinction himself between belief in tutelary spirits and belief in the One Life (as indeed Coleridge would not have done so easily), he maintains nonetheless that 'The trouble about Wordsworth's spirits is that they are so evidently fanciful': 'because of their sub-classical associations', they 'are hard to take very seriously' (1984: 40).

In Jonathan's late twentieth-century opinion, 'we react not as to an expression of faith in supernatural powers, but as to a figurative way of saying that in his (for the period) very surprising view, it was the painful moments of a happy childhood that had been most formative' (Wordsworth 1979b: 573-4). Personally, I find the poetry weaker if these spirits are given 'something of the force of metaphor' (1984: 40). I prefer to return to Ernest de Selincourt's early twentieth-century interpretation:

> when Wordsworth began to write *The Prelude* he still delighted to conceive of Nature not merely as the expression

> of one divine spirit, but as in its several parts animated by individual spirits who had, like human beings, an independent life and power of action. This was obviously his firm belief in the primitive paganism of his boyhood; and long after he had given up definite belief in it, he cherished it as more than mere poetic fancy. (Wordsworth 1928: 506)

I believe that the literariness of the following passage from Wordsworth's early draft of *The Prelude* can be reconciled with the vitality of spiritual entities; that which Jonathan Wordsworth derides as the 'artificiality' of the invocation is in fact part of its power:

> Ye Powers of earth! ye Genii of the springs!
> And ye that have your voices in the clouds
> And ye that are familiars of the lakes
> And standing pools. ah! not for trivial ends
> Through snow and sunshine, through the sparkling plains
> Of moonlight frost and in the stormy day
> Did ye with such assiduous love pursue
> Your favourite and your joy. I may not think
> A vulgar hope was yours when ye employed
> Such ministry, when ye through many a year
> Thus by the agency of boyish sports
> On caves and trees, upon the woods and hills,
> Impressed upon all forms the characters
> Of danger or desire, and thus did make
> The surface of the universal earth
> With meanings of delight, of hope and fear
> Work like a sea. (1977: 22-3 and 250-3)

Wordsworth's 'familiars of the Lakes' (1977: 125; the l is capitalized the first time Wordsworth elaborates on this line in Dorothy's notebook) are supernatural spirits that abide in the

Lake District. When he composed these lines, as we have seen in Chapter 1, Wordsworth was isolated in Germany during the coldest winter of the eighteenth century. Unable to begin the much cherished project of a long philosophical poem, the poet was homesick for his native hills, and he probably understood with Agrippa that there are in every region specific kinds of spirits: 'Hence it is that the choice of a place, region, or time doth much conduce to the happiness of life where any one shall dwell, and frequent, according to the nature and instinct of his own Genius' (2004: 532). Writing about his childhood in the Lakes while invoking the spirits of that region, the poet may well have been planning his return there in order to complete his life's work with their help. Since such powers have educated him as a child of their region, he is most suited to be conducted by them advantageously again if he returns to that spot.

That Wordsworth's 'familiars' are also of 'standing pools' confirms that his apostrophe draws on Prospero's renunciation speech in *The Tempest*, another region that *genii* inhabit. Wordsworth's deliberate allusion to Shakespeare discloses his fancy that the guardian spirits of his childhood, the tutelary spirits of specific spots, that is, lakes, hills and groves in Cumbria where he grew up, have migrated to spots in his remembering of the English canon, in order to take care of the older poet. Perhaps, like Ariel in *The Tempest*, each of Wordsworth's personifying spirits has the ability to be almost in two kinds of places at once. Perhaps Wordsworth's boyhood love of books in the context of his native hills effected the transmission.

Wordsworth will return as an adult to the Lakes, literally, very soon after his return to England in 1799, but he can also return there imaginatively and creatively beforehand. It is hoped in both cases that, as Agrippa says of 'solary men' in a 'solary region', 'by the present aid of' his 'advantageous conductors or Genii', the poet 'shall be brought beyond expectation, and their own power, to happy events' (2004: 524). Such guardians are at once outside and inside the growing boy and outside and inside the adult's poem; they move to the boy from his surroundings, the 'hils, brooks, standing lakes & groves' of the Lake District, moving thus through recorded 'spots of time' to *The Prelude*. But they are also to be found in the passages that connect those episodes, migrating to the poem from its fields of literary allusion and influence, the spots where *The Prelude* has been nurtured in the poet's at once imitative and original imagination, specifically here, the 'hils, brooks, standing lakes & groves' of Prospero's speech:

> Ye Elves of hils, brooks, standing lakes & groves,
> And ye that on the sands with printlesse foote
> Do chase the ebbing-*Neptune*, and doe flie him
> When he comes backe: you demy-Puppets, that
> By Moon-shine doe the greene sowre Ringlets make,
> Whereof the Ewe not bites: and you, whose pastime
> Is to make midnight-Mushrumps, that rejoice
> To heare the solemn Curfewe, by whose ayde
> (Weake Masters though ye be) I have bedymn'd
> The Noone-tide Sun, call'd forth the mutinous windes,
> And twixt the greene Sea, and the azur'd vault
> Set roaring warre: To the dread ratling Thunder
> Have I given fire, and rifted *Joves* stowt Oke
> With his owne Bolt: The strong bass'd promontorie
> Have I made shake, and by the spurs pluckt up
> The pyne, and Cedar. Graves at my command
> Have wak'd their sleepers, op'd, and let 'em forth
> By my so potent Art. But this rough Magicke
> I here abjure: and when I have requir'd
> Some heavenly Musicke (which even now I do)
> To worke mine end upon their Sences, that
> This Ayrie-charme is for, I'le breake my staffe,
> Bury it certaine fadomes in the earth,
> And deeper then did ever Plummet sound

Ile drowne my booke.
Solemne musicke. (V. i. 33-57)

Wordsworth, a poet about to embark on his life's work, while undergoing a temporary exile from his homeland, remembers his childhood superstitions and invokes spirits from his birthplace as well as English literature. He alludes to a speech, in which a magus, about to return home, is renouncing his control over spirits that he discovered on the island of his exile, through his knowledge of esoteric literature.

Prospero's speech is, in turn, an imitation of a famous passage to do with magic from classical literature, Medea's invocation in Book Seven of Ovid's *Metamorphoses*:

Ye Ayres and windes: ye Elves of Hilles, of Brookes, of Woods alone,
Of standing Lakes, and of the Night approche ye everychone.
Through helpe of whom (the crooked bankes much wondring at the thing)
I have compelled streames to run cleane backward to their spring.
By charmes I make the calme Seas rough, and make ye rough seas plain
And cover all the Skie with Cloudes, and chase them thence againe.
By charmes I rayse and lay the windes, and burst the Vipers jaw,
And from the bowels of the Earth both stones and trees doe drawe.
Whole woods and Forestes I remove: I make the Mountaines shake,
And even the Earth it selfe to grone and fearfully to quake.
I call up dead men from their graves: and thee O lightsome Moone

> I darken oft, though beaten brasse abate thy peril soone.
> Our Sorcerie dimmes the Morning faire, and darkes ye Sun at Noone. (VII. 265-77)

The witch who speaks these lines would have been regarded as wicked, in both Ovid's and Shakespeare's times, because her transgressive magic, like science today, interferes with the natural order. As she makes this invocation Medea is out gathering herbs by moonlight in order to rejuvenate her father-in-law, her one pious act among a litany of wicked ones. Jonathan Bate infers that Ovid thus 'finds some soul of goodness in things evil. The question with regard to Prospero's magic is whether the opposite applies: is there some soul of darkness in his white magic' (1994: 251)?

Like many modern critics I see that Prospero is an inscrutable, complex and potentially ambivalent, even thwarted, character. But I see no reason not to agree with Frank Kermode when he argues that this mage is specifically 'a theurgist, whose Art is to achieve supremacy over the natural world by holy magic': 'His object is to "walk to the skie", as Vaughan puts it, before death, by ascending through the created worlds to the condition of angels' (1987: xl and xli). On the other hand, Medea's witchcraft pertains to goety: her magic could be called 'natural' because it exploits universal sympathies, but it is, in fact, highly unnatural: it relies on the invocation and employment of the lower orders of demons to disturb natural processes.

Shakespeare skillfully imitates Ovid by translating and elaborating certain details of Medea's invocation, using both Ovid's original Latin and Arthur Golding's translation quoted above; the choice of text itself, a *locus classicus* of witchcraft in the Renaissance, and most of Shakespeare's amplifications, make Prospero's well-intended white magic seem spotted with black. Most damningly of all, Prospero's speech reveals for the first time in the play that he is, like Medea, a necromancer. As Bate has argued,

> The capacity to raise the dead… is the final mark of the potency of Prospero's art. It is also a sign of its roughness and a reason for its abjuration…. Whereas Medea goes on using her magic to act out revenge plots, Prospero renounces his and in so doing marks a movement away from the pagan world towards Christian 'kindness'. Medea's powers are summoned up not so that they can be exercised, but so that they can be rejected. (1994: 252)

Knowledge of the source would have been integral to an understanding of Prospero's speech, in the early seventeenth century, as it is again in academic circles today. Shakespeare would have expected audiences to compare or contrast Prospero and Medea.

Today we like to think of Wordsworth as an inspired poet, creating spontaneously original poetry, unlike Shakespeare who relied so much on imitation. Perhaps that is why Wordsworth's apostrophes to 'Powers', 'Genii' and 'Familiars' in early versions of *The Prelude* disturb modern critics. Repeatedly, the adult poet addresses the same kinds of supernatural beings that his younger self had fancied he'd felt during and after moments of stress in the Lakes, drawing happily on similar invocations in Akenside, Shakespeare and others as he does so. As Bate acknowledges, 'Miltonic and eighteenth-century invocations, other catalogues of "ye"s, have intervened between Shakespeare and *The Prelude*' (1989: 109). When we hear these echoes resound in Wordsworth's poem, are we witnessing, then, a poet deploying a lazy, very late Renaissance, style of imitation, imitating even imitations? Does Wordsworth appropriate other poems without the skill to be found in Shakespeare's suggestive elaborations of Ovid? Or does his mode of allusion differ radically from Shakespeare's style of imitation?

On this occasion, Bate would argue, 'close parallels of phraseology inevitably make the reader recall Prospero' (1989: 109). Wordsworth must have intended that Coleridge, to whom *The*

Prelude is primarily addressed, notice the allusion to Shakespeare in 'ye that are Familiars of the lakes | And standing pools'. Nonetheless, the idea that Wordsworth is highly original and not dependent on predecessors dates back as far as Coleridge's assessment of the poet: 'in imaginative power, he stands nearest of all modern writers to Shakespear and Milton; and yet in a kind perfectly unborrowed and his own' (1983: 2. 151). Bate acknowledges that Coleridge's:

> summing up of Wordsworth's pre-eminent gift remains definitive.... But 'perfectly unborrowed' is wrong, for Wordsworth at his best borrows creatively. Certain inherited phrases, especially those associated with passages that exemplify or circumscribe 'imaginative power' ...are powerful ghostly presences that enable Wordsworth to *stand near* to Shakespeare and Milton in a different way from that meant by Coleridge. (1989: 116)

Bate makes Wordsworth sound almost like a necromancer, at the very least a medium. To what degree do these 'inherited phrases' embody the 'ghostly presences' of the dead poets themselves? Should we take the critic's argument literally? In that case, Wordsworth's poetry performs before us that of which Prospero boasts: 'Graves at my command | Have wak'd their sleepers, op'd, and let 'em forth | By my so potent Art'. Is this the final mark of the potency of Wordsworth's art? Is it also a sign of its roughness and a reason for its abjuration? Or is such magic, confined within literature, beneficent? Wordsworth's allusions call on Shakespeare and Milton, 'done with the contests of life, and by prowess of soul become daemons' (Milton 2007a: 179), and these 'powerful ghostly presences' become his 'personifying spirits', that is, the 'Gates and Gate-keepers' (1980: 272) to his own soul-making journey at the beginning of *The Prelude*.

I detect a perhaps unwitting ambiguity in the critic Bate's

description of the poet's practice of allusion. Does Wordsworth borrow creatively phrases that he has already inherited? T. S. Eliot understood that tradition 'cannot be inherited, and if you want it you must obtain it by great labour' (1986: 14), but I think that he was only half right: the great labour is to claim your inheritance. The poet must borrow from others that which is already his, just as Dante must journey through *Purgatorio*, 'to return another time to where I am' (II. 91-2); Wordsworth's callings to earlier poets allow him to be greater than he knows: in Upton's words, 'The essence of the spiritual Path is to travel to where we already live, to become what we are' (2008: 56).

Bate explains that 'humanist imitation was based on the premiss that classical texts were appropriate patterns or models because they embodied fundamental, enduring truths' (1994: 9). Is Romantic allusion based on the premise that certain phrases or passages of precursor poets can be borrowed because they embody the 'ghostly presences' of their makers? I am conjuring an argument by conversing with two books by Bate, one on Shakespeare and Ovid, the other on the Romantics and Shakespeare, because I am interested in Wordsworth's transformations of standard humanist procedures of literary imitation. For Bate, Renaissance imitation often amounts to allusion: 'the source text is *brought into play* (from Latin *al-ludo*, to play with); its presence does significant aesthetic work of a sort which cannot be performed by a submerged source' (1994: 10). When Wordsworth brings source texts into play what kind of work do their presences perform, what kind of powers do they have? Or contain?

At the beginning of early versions of *The Prelude*, Wordsworth does not just describe his childhood belief in spiritual beings; he invokes such spirits to help him on his way to where he already is. Thus elves, powers, genii, and familiars flock to his poem. That his invocations contain allusions to Shakespeare and later poets should be taken as proof that such beings can also reside in works of literature as well as in the features in a landscape. They have homes in the topoi of poems as well as in the topography of our diminishing countryside. Perhaps industrial urbanization and burgeoning local scepticism have forced these spirits to reside more often in the friendlier environment of our literature. The dead also walk Wordsworth's poetry in the manner that Milton's attendant spirit comes down from Heaven to tend on mortal thoughts. The souls of dead poets that have become guardian spirits attend those living who have also embarked creatively on the spiritual path. When Wordsworth brings source texts into play he revives certain phrases into powerful ghostly presences to do significant work for him: they seem to be outside the ordinary self but they open a gate to a greater self within of which they are part.

Such spirits serve their purpose most powerfully at the very moment of their vanishing. We invoke them to dismiss them within. Like Prospero, Wordsworth calls to his guardian spirits and familiars (Shakespeare and other poets as well as the elves or genii he believed in as a child) in order to move to the next stage of his soul-making journey when he will no longer have such need of them. Kermode sees that Prospero's magic is 'rough' because, 'Expressing itself in the manipulation of material forces', it is 'unsubtle by comparison with the next degree of the mage's enlightenment' (Shakespeare 1987: 115). Wordsworth's later revisions to the apostrophes that we have been explicating so far in this chapter prove that he too is attempting to move to a greater degree of enlightenment. That Wordsworth falls to the side of his spiritual journey, failing to complete creatively the task that is begun with *The Prelude*, has nothing to do with scepticism.

By 1805 Wordsworth still believed that 'The mind of man is framed even like the breath | And harmony of music', but the different kinds of Spirits have vanished from the subsequent lines of poetry, for he continues:

There is a dark
Invisible workmanship that reconciles
Discordant elements, and makes them move
In one society. (*1805 Prelude*, I. 352-6)

The text that was finally published in 1850 is even darker:

Dust as we are, the immortal spirit grows
Like harmony in music; there is a dark
Inscrutable workmanship that reconciles
Discordant elements, makes them cling together
In one society. (*1850 Prelude*, I. 340-4)

The fellowship of 'Spirits' becomes an 'Invisible' and then an 'Inscrutable workmanship'. When 'Discordant elements' 'cling together' they seem more desperate than when they 'move together'.

The passage of 'ye's with its allusion to Prospero's speech undergoes revisions too. One of the 1799 manuscripts, in Dorothy's hand, is full of crossings out at this point of the poem, proving that Wordsworth was at pains to distance himself from Shakespeare: 'Ye Powers of earth! ye Genii of the springs!' and the next five lines, including 'ye that are familiars of the lakes | And standing pools' are deleted and replaced with 'Ye winds ye voices that were in the clouds | Ye visions of the mountains Virtues, powers' (1977: 250-3). Wordsworth was trying to organize Prospero's pagan genii according to medieval angelology. By 1805 the passage had assumed almost its final form:

Ye Presences of Nature, in the sky
Or on the earth! Ye Visions of the hills!
And Souls of lonely places! can I think
A vulgar hope was yours when Ye employ'd

> Such ministry, [when] Ye through many a year
> Haunting me thus among my boyish sports,
> On caves and trees, upon the woods and hills,
> Impress'd upon all forms the characters
> Of danger or desire, and thus did make
> The surface of the universal earth
> With triumph, and delight, and hope, and fear,
> Work like a sea. (*1805 Prelude*, I. 491-502)

Perhaps the 'Ye', capitalized here, is enough to conjure Shakespeare, as well as powers, genii and familiars. The powerful ghostly presence of the precursor poet has been veiled, and the suggestion of different orders of angels has been replaced, by 'Souls of lonely places', or ordinary local ghosts doomed to wander certain spots of Cumbria as part of their Purgatory.

Like Prospero at the end of his project, Wordsworth has invoked certain kinds of spirits, in order to renounce his dealings with them. They should be substituted for that which already contains them. Like Augustine at the beginning of his *Confessions*, Wordsworth's revisions to his autobiographical poem reveal him wondering about the paradox of invoking that power, which is always already in man:

> And how shall I call upon my God, my Lord and God? because that when I invoke him, I call him into myself: and what place is there in me fit for my God to come into me by, whither God may come into me; even that God which made heaven and earth? Is it so, my Lord God? Is there anything in me which can contain thee? Nay, can both heaven and earth which thou hast made, and in which thou hast made me, in any wise contain thee? Or else because whatsoever is, could not subsist without thee, must it follow thereupon, that whatsoever hath being, is endued with a capacity of thee? (2002: 1. 5; I. ii)

God is in man, and man in God. Such insight comes to those who would return home, 'where | Every third thought shall be my grave' (*The Tempest*, V. i. 310-1). Wordsworth's and Prospero's 'Ye's must become the more intimate and more mysterious 'thee' of Augustine's beautiful meditation on invocation. If 'We say God and the imagination are one' (Stevens 1954: 524), how do poems call upon that power already within man? How do we awake creatively to know that we each contain that which contains all? Both Augustine and Prospero understand that they must look after: each will record 'The story of my life, | And the particular accidents, gon by | Since I came to this Isle' (*The Tempest*, V. i. 304-6), but then each must consider the future. (It seems that Milan is a city of significance in different ways for both theologian-bishop and mage-duke.) Wordsworth worries me because he becomes so consumed by the story of his life in *The Prelude*, so obsessed with what comes before, that he neglects to develop his capacity to look after, his 'capacity of thee', or that which comes to us from the future. Can our '*Indulgence*' (*The Tempest*, 'Epilogue', 20) set the poet free as audiences have prayed and clapped for Prospero?

With the help of her familiars Medea has 'compelled streames to run cleane backward to their spring.' When a stream runs backwards, a natural process is quite literally reversed; a backward-running stream is a fit symbol for the soul-making activity of any life. Each must walk upstream to find our eternal source in God. When Wordsworth elaborates his 'spots of time' one is tempted to think that he walks back up the river of his life, as he worked backwards through Dorothy's German notebook, but such attention to his memories of past experience is to drift downwards to the sea of time and space.

The motif of a river running backwards can also help us to think about the relations between Ovid, Shakespeare and Wordsworth. Conventional theories about imitation, allusion and influence see relatively uncomplicated causal relationships between each text. Shakespeare has imitated Ovid and this new work, in turn, influences Wordsworth. That is indisputable; this chapter has presented most of the evidence. But is there another kind of influence, a supernatural inflowing, which would compel this stream of conventional literary influence to run clean backwards to its spring? If influence runs backwards then all of these texts flow to the same supernatural source. Each text calls to supernatural powers that reverse conventional or natural processes of influence.

Coleridge continued his 1798 appraisal, which Hazlitt recorded, of the spirits in, or the spirit of, Wordsworth's poetry, by conceding that 'his philosophic poetry had a grand and comprehensive spirit in it, so that his soul seemed to inhabit the universe like a palace, and to discover truth by intuition, rather than by deduction' (Hazlitt 1982: 58). At his greatest moments, Wordsworth does look forward to eternity, and that is partly why I love him. But his mistake, metaphysically speaking, despite the very moving and very beautiful poetry that comes out of his decision to do so, is to look backwards for so long at past experience in *The Prelude*. Then again, there are moments when his work can compel the supernatural to come to it from the future and grow to a point without which the poetry cannot even begin. As you have probably gathered by now, I cannot shake my deeply ambivalent feelings about Wordsworth.

The one-in-many and the many-in-one

A supernatural being vanishes into Blake's 'Introduction' to *Songs of Innocence*:

> Piping down the valleys wild
> Piping songs of pleasant glee
> On a cloud I saw a child.
> And he laughing said to me.

Pipe a song about a Lamb;
So I piped with merry chear,
Piper pipe that song again –
So I piped, he wept to hear.

Drop thy pipe thy happy pipe
Sing thy songs of happy chear,
So I sung the same again,
While he wept with joy to hear

Piper sit thee down and write
In a book that all may read –
So he vanish'd from my sight.
And I pluck'd a hollow reed.

And I made a rural pen,
And I stain'd the water clear,
And I wrote my happy songs,
Every child may joy to hear (Plate 4)

This poem is at once happy and sad. When the child on the cloud disappears, where does he go? Blake's 'rural pen' is at once an old-fashioned kind of writing instrument and a fold or enclosure for spirits of the countryside. His pen provides them with a new home as the world becomes more industrialized and their habitat is made into housing estates and shopping malls.

Blake's 'Introduction' is made to be 'a window open in Heaven', not a leaden rain cloud, but a way of looking into 'the golden age' (Blake 2002: xxix). The enclosure of poetry turns out to be an opening through which the 'Industrious' (Blake, *Milton*, Plate 35. 43) can converse with 'Paradise' (Blake 2008: 559). The putto enters Blake's body of work through this window as a guardian spirit that becomes the soul of Blake's work. Any soul that enters a body may become baffled by its new state, but its task is to make itself greater than it knows, by disciplining its everyday self, like any reader or writer of poetry. This project is more fully realized by the time of Blake's prophetic poem, *Milton*, completed around twenty years' later in about 1811.

This same process is also occurring in the body of all of our poetry. Supernatural forms that might be perceived as merely quaint neoclassical figures from the middle and end of our Renaissance are growing up into a potent spiritual being, or 'moving soul' (Wordsworth, *1805 Prelude*, XIII. 171), within what we call the canon: the many-in-one and the one-in-many. Such is the spirit of poetry that I would delineate in this book. The body of work that we call the canon can only articulate by obscurely enfolding its more than human meaning; apprehension of 'bright eternal Self' (Yeats and Swami 1970: 135), stained or penned in poems, makes humans 'feel that we are greater than we know' (Wordsworth 2009: 3. 363): poetry is a spotted way of acknowledging that each of us contains that which is always spotless, as Blake understood in the 'Introduction' to his body of work. The putto that is penned in Blake's poem points to a moment in poetry that can transform its spotted readers from the future. As Rainer Maria Rilke said a hundred or so years after Blake:

> We cannot say who has come, perhaps we shall never know, but there are many indications that it is the future that enters into us like this, in order to be transformed within us, long before it actually occurs. (2011: 52)

Supernatural forms have a habit of entering a country's literature when its oral culture is dying out and the population becomes more urban and sceptical. In England, genii have flocked to our literature from the sixteenth century onwards. When Yeats was recording the last vestiges of ancient traditions in Ireland during the late nineteenth century, the fairies began to find a new home in his verse. I can well imagine that the response of most people today to these wild paragraphs will be close to that of Theseus to the events of *A Midsummer-Night's Dream*:

I never may beleeve
These anticke fables, nor these Fairy toyes.
Lovers and mad men have such seething braines,
Such shaping phantasies, that apprehend more
Than coole reason ever comprehends.
The Lunaticke, the Lover, and the Poet,
Are of imagination all compact.
One sees more divels than vaste hell can hold;
That is the mad man. The Lover, all as franticke,
Sees *Helens* beauty in a brow of *Egipt*.
The Poets eye, in a fine frenzy rolling, doth glance
From heaven to earth, from earth to heaven.
And as imagination bodies forth the forms of things
Unknowne; the Poets pen turnes them to shapes,
And gives to aire nothing, a locall habitation,
And a name. (V. i. 2-17)

But the joke is on Theseus. Shakespeare is employing dramatic irony here, since the audience by now knows more than this rather literal minded personage perceives. In terms of the reality of the play we know that fairies are real since we have witnessed them talking and manipulating action. It is also strange that Theseus does not believe in 'anticke', that is, antic or antique, 'fables' since he is manifestly a part of their reality. Theseus, in a rather ignorant manner, does not believe in the reality of his own play or even the larger reality of classical mythology, which guarantees his presence in the play. When we refuse to believe in the supernatural are we in the same unfortunate position as Theseus? Is there a whole globe of spirits, a universal theatre of the supernatural, now laughing or half-aghast at our inhibiting scepticism, our refusal to believe in what we cannot sense?

Hippolyta's response to such scepticism proves her to be more sensitive and intelligent, less provincial in her spiritual outlook, than her new husband:

> But all the storie of the night told over,
> And all their minds transfigur'd so together,
> More witnesseth than fancies images,
> And growes to something of great constancie;
> But howsoever, strange, and admirable. (V. i. 23-7)

She 'thinks like a police detective (a role Theseus might have relished)', as A. D. Nuttall has argued, and appeals to what will be called, in the twentieth century, 'the coherence theory of truth': 'if the witnesses separately tell stories that form a consistent whole, they are likely to be telling the truth' (2007: 123). Hippolyta appeals to such a theory precisely because it will appeal to Theseus, if he really thought about the matter; she has already worked out how to get around her husband by thinking ahead of him. Since she knows that she is merely keeping one step ahead of scepticism, she also knows, crucially, the limits of her theory.

Many of us today sound like that ignorant stick, Theseus, but for different reasons, and so we will do well to listen to the whole of his wise wife's argument. Common-sense, like Theseus, is sceptical about accounts of fairies because it abides by a narrow understanding of 'the correspondence theory, which says a statement is true if it corresponds with a certain fact'. Others discredit belief in the supernatural by stretching Hippolyta's very theory of coherence, 'which says a statement is true if it can be "verified" – in the sense, "shown to be harmonious" – with the larger belief system (in practice, the other statements we make)' (Nuttall 2007: 123). Many intellectuals at university will cheerfully tell you that all you hold to be true is constructed by what we say, and thus transcendental meaning is a fiction. Intent to know only their social selves, students of literature have figured out that the coherence theory of truth implies that all in which we believe is contingent: belief systems are ideologies that can now be deconstructed.

However, having grasped the coherence theory of truth before it was invented, Hippolyta nonetheless checks herself. She thinks beyond future readers who have developed this theory into just another way of being sceptical in the world. By questioning her husband's assumptions, and then by questioning her own questioning, the Queen of the Amazons also appeals to and undermines all of our contemporary theories about reality and language. Nuttall offers a convincing gloss of that crucial last line of hers, 'But howsoever, strange, and admirable': '"Although I have stressed the consistency [constancie] of these accounts and urged that this consistency could ripen into truth status, I don't want to deny that the events of the night, seen now not as internally related to one another but as a whole, are utterly strange, a matter for wonder"' (2007: 124). If only literary theorists after Jacques Derrida had entertained such a caveat, university departments across the humanities would not be in such postmodernist disarray today.

I am interested in Hippolyta's monumentally significant 'But howsoever'. How does the coherence of a work look after its essential incoherence? Maurice Blanchot's theories about narration help me to think about how that which excites wonder in a work can stand firm in our minds: 'Narration [*Le récit*] is not the account of an event but the event itself, its imminence, the site where it will occur – it is a happening about to happen whose magnetic power may enable the narration to happen' (1992: 62). Likewise in poems, supernatural beings are not just described; they are invoked by the text, which is now the site where they can occur, their imminence. Like the relation of God and the imagination, as Timothy Clark explains, 'Topologically, the movement between this *récit* and its event is that of a spiral whose spiralling inwards is ceaseless, asymptotic' (1992: 86).

Narration is movement towards:

> a point which is not only unknown, ignored and strange but such that it seems to have no prior reality apart from this movement, yet is so compulsive that narration's appeal depends on it to the extent that it cannot even 'begin' before it has reached it, while it is only the narration and the unpredictable movement of the narration which provide the space where this point becomes real, powerful and appealing. (Blanchot 1992: 62)

The coherence of any account cannot be separated from the essential incoherence of its event. When the supernatural is invoked in a work, text and genius, the poem and its familiar, obey the same law of movement as narration and event. Blanchot deepens our understanding of the correspondence theory of truth by making it emerge out of a crisis that the coherence theory of truth must suffer during narration. Hippolyta's 'But howsoever', at once separating and joining constancy and strangeness, is essential to the validity of any story or poem; as Nuttall says, 'we sense unfinished business' (2007: 124): fairies find their proper home half-created when each witness perceives them, through whose records, assembled together, we recognize the true strangeness of our world.

How does 'something of great constancie', for example, Shakespeare's *Complete Works* or the canon of English literature, apprehend that which is 'strange, and admirable'? Can it be that fancy's images, for example, late eighteenth-century descriptions of fairies, grow to something of great constancy within a play or poem? In the past most people believed in fairies and so, as numerous accounts testify, fairies were often witnessed. If a work makes us believe in fairies, even temporarily, do they thus come into existence within that work whenever it is read with most believing mind, however strange that seems?

Before our late modern period literature was full of supernatural beings. In *Paradise Lost,* Adam explains to Eve in Eden:

> Millions of spiritual Creatures walk the Earth
> Unseen, both when we wake, and when we sleep:
> All these with ceasless praise his works behold
> Both day and night: how often from the steep
> Of echoing Hill or Thicket have we heard
> Celestial voices to the midnight air,
> Sole, or responsive each to others note
> Singing thir great Creator: oft in bands
> While they keep watch, or nightly rounding walk,
> With Heav'nly touch of instrumental sounds
> In full harmonic number joind, thir songs
> Divide the night, and lift our thoughts to Heaven. (IV. 677-88)

Milton is not invoking these spiritual creatures (he has already called upon his 'Heav'nly Muse' at the beginning of the poem), but he is drawing on Hesiod's invocation of the Muses at the beginning of his *Theogony*:

> Let us begin to sing from the Heliconian Muses, who possess the great and holy mountain of Helicon and dance on their soft feet around the violet-dark fountain and the altar of Cronus' mighty son... and after they have washed their tender skin... they perform choral dances.... Starting out from there, shrouded in thick invisibility, by night they walk, sending forth their very beautiful voice[.]

One day they came to the shepherd Hesiod in the fields and taught him beautiful song, but warning him meanwhile: '"Field-dwelling shepherds, ignoble disgraces, mere bellies: we know how to say many false things similar to genuine ones, but we know, when we wish, how to proclaim true things'". The Muses 'breathed a divine voice' into Hesiod, commanding him 'to sing of the race of blessed ones who always are, but always to sing of themselves first and last'. The shepherd-poet understood his responsibility because great poems 'begin from the Muses, who by singing for their father Zeus give pleasure to his great mind within Olympus, telling of what is and what will be and what was before, harmonizing in their sound' (see *Theogony*, 1-34).

I am concerned about how such divine powers cohere in any poem during our sceptical late modern age. Rather depressingly, E. R. Curtius asserted in the twentieth century, 'For us the Muses are shadowy figures of a tradition that has long since had its day' (1990: 228). Can this really be true? As the many-in-one and the one-in-many, the daughters of Zeus are that strange point towards which a poem moves so that it may begin, such unpredictable movement providing the space where such powers are invoked to call on us. If they are 'shadowy figures' today, they should be treated with due care. The Muses that inspired Hesiod, breathing into him a divine voice, are the same 'forces of the intermediary plane or psychic realm' that Wordsworth invoked in the first drafts of *The Prelude*. Perhaps both Hesiod and Wordsworth have succumbed somewhat to 'the superhuman glamour with which the Regime of Nature can sometimes clothe the… poet'.

Milton's description of the situation in which Adam tells Eve of spiritual creatures is significant: 'Thus talking hand in hand alone they pass'd | On to thir blissful Bower' (IV. 689-90). This moment foreshadows the very end of the poem, after Adam and Eve have been led hastily out of Paradise, 'and down the Cliff as fast | To the subjected Plaine':

They looking back, all th' Eastern side beheld
Of Paradise, so late thir happie seat,
Wav'd over by that flaming Brand, the Gate
With dreadful Faces throng'd and fierie Armes:

> Som natural tears they drop'd, but wip'd them soon;
> The World was all before them, where to choose
> Thir place of rest, and Providence thir guide:
> They hand in hand with wandring steps and slow,
> Through *Eden* took thir solitarie way. (XII. 639-40 and 641-9)

The spiritual watchmen are now visible and silent; their new task is to prevent our first parents from returning to their original home. Without their spiritual guard Adam and Eve, 'hand in hand', are guided by providence: they must trust in the foreknowledge and protective care of God.

We are still today taking our solitary way beneath the fiery cliffs of Paradise; only we are more alone at the moment than we ever were:

> the psychological dangers through which earlier generations were guided by the symbols and spiritual exercises of their mythological and religious inheritance, we today (in so far as we are unbelievers, or, if believers, in so far as our inherited beliefs fail to represent the real problems of contemporary life) must face alone, or, at best, with only tentative, impromptu, and not often very effective guidance. This is our problem as modern, 'enlightened' individuals, for whom all gods and devils have been rationalized out of existence.

Joseph Campbell understood that 'we may yet see delineated something of our still human course' 'in the multitude of myths and legends that have been preserved to us'. I would add that the greatest poetry of the modern period could provide us with requisite spiritual guidance if it is read aright. 'To hear and profit, however, one may have to submit somehow to purgation and surrender. And that is part of our problem: just how to do that. "Or do you think that ye shall enter the Garden of Bliss without such trials as came to those who passed away before you"' (1993: 104 and 105)?

It may be that we recognize a certain threshold to be crossed in what is created, half out of this world, in the exalted language of poetry, painting and music; when life on earth is thus transformed by art, we perceive this dim spot to be peopled by spiritual helpers. Before the Fall, God created 'Millions of spiritual Creatures' as man's guard on earth; after the Fall, each half-creates what can be perceived, and that is possibly the guide we recognize 'In nature and the language of the sense' (Wordsworth 2009: 1. 375). Proust finds a kind of spiritual discipline in creative work just as his narrator derives joy from his first hearing of pieces of music:

> I liked to fix my thoughts only upon what was still obscure to me, and to be able, in the course of these successive renderings, thanks to the increasing but, alas, distorting and alien light of my intellect, to link to one another the fragmentary and interrupted lines of the structure which at first had been almost hidden in a mist. (1996: 5. 424-4)

Coherence is in love with incoherence just as the freshest truth is only found in the most furtive fiction. How does one submit to purgation and surrender? Proust talks of 'Experimental faith':

> It is life that, little by little, case by case, enables us to observe that what is most important to our hearts or to our minds is taught us not by reasoning but by other powers. And then it is the intelligence itself, which acknowledging their superiority, abdicates to them through reasoning and consents to become their collaborator and their servant. (1996: 5. 482)

Proust seems to be describing a process akin to Wordsworth's inspiration during the early phases of writing *The Prelude*: the poet calls to 'other powers' of supernatural origin and becomes 'their collaborator and their servant'. It may be, however, that 'Experimental faith' is too retrogressive. I am suspicious of the long backward looks to past experiences that both Wordsworth and Proust take in their masterpieces. The greatest art looks after not just before.

Blake, whose art looks more often courageously forward to eternity that comes to us out of the future, understood that angels are the powers hidden in the faculties and organs of man:

> The ancient Poets animated all sensible objects with Gods or Geniuses, calling them by the names and adorning them with the properties of woods, rivers, mountains, lakes, cities, nations, and whatever their enlarged & numerous senses could perceive.
>
> And particularly they studied the genius of each city & country. placing it under its mental deity.
>
> Till a system was formed, which some took advantage of & enslav'd the vulgar by attempting to realize or abstract the mental deities from their objects: thus began Priesthood.
>
> Choosing forms of worship from poetic tales.
>
> And at length they pronounced that the Gods had orderd such things.
>
> Thus men forgot that All deities reside in the human breast. (*The Marriage of Heaven and Hell*, Plate 11)

According to Harold Bloom, here Blake 'explains how the priests or Angels came into existence to oppose the poets or Devils. This process is one of codifying poetry into scripture, and now calls forth its contrary in Blake's Bible of Hell, or poems restoring orthodox scriptures into their primal imaginative forms' (Blake 2008: 898). As Suheil Bushrui acknowledges, 'The interior search is... the means by which truth will be discovered'. Poetry that articulates the learning of the imagination allows each to discover each day new regions in the soul:

> Imagination for Blake is more than the limited sense of the poet's 'muse,' but rather creates the inspiration and knowledge of not the arts alone, but of all deeper intuitions. Blake held the belief, dangerously heterodox at the time, that these deepest intuitions, expressed through the religious impulse, meant that all religions are fundamentally one: 'The Religions of all Nations are derived from each Nation's different reception of the Poetic Genius, which is everywhere call'd the Spirit of Prophecy… As all men are alike (tho' infinitely various), So all Religions &, as all similars, have one source.' (2008: 106; quoting from Blake's *All Religions are One*, Principles 5 and 7)

Georg Trakl's poem 'Jahr' or 'Year' allows a god or guardian spirit to cohere in language in order to take up its proper residence 'in the human breast'. Written about one hundred years ago, it receives 'the Poetic Genius' or 'the Spirit of Prophecy' for our time:

> Dark silence of childhood. Under young green ashtrees
> Meekness broods with bluish glance; golden peace.
> A dark thing delights in the fragrance of violets; swaying ears
> of corn
> At evening, seeds and the golden shades of melancholy.
> Beams are hewn by the carpenter; in the twilit vale
> The mill grinds; a scarlet mouth swells amid hazel leaves,
> Manly red bowed over silent waters.
> Quiet is the autumn, the spirit of the forest; golden cloud
> Follows the solitary man, the grandson's black shadow.
> Decline in the room of stone; the night images of tears
> Are gathered at the source under ancient cypresses;
> Golden eye of inception, dark patience of the end. (2001: 95)

When I picture this poem, and it is hard not to, then I think of the poet as taking elements from various late nineteenth-century and early twentieth-century art movements. It has the vivid colouring of a Fauvist painting, contains the archetypal resonances of symbolist canvasses, and attains to the religious intensity of Van Gogh's mature works. It moves in words beyond the confines of Expressionism. In fact, Trakl described his poetic style as 'my pictorial manner which forges together four separate image-parts in four lines of a stanza into a single impression'. As his English translator, Alexander Stillmark explains, 'This serial style is essentially cumulative in that it builds up its effects from discrete elements of language and these are generally marked from each other by a period which coincides with the end of a line'. Like Poe, Baudelaire and Rimbaud before him, Trakl immersed himself in the dregs of this dim spot, deriving 'inspiration from what is decadent corrupt and morbid' in this dark world and wide (Trakl 2001: xiv and xii). The situation of 'the solitary man' followed by a golden cloud seems to me a young man's intensification of the plight of our first parents on the dark plains below the flaming gates of Paradise.

Despite the poet's unflinching representation of 'Decline in the room of stone', or life today on this earth that will become our sarcophagus, I believe that his poem allows a supernatural being to come to presence as a gate-keeper to realms of imaginative possibility within. The poem begins by looking back to 'Dark silence of childhood', but it is about a new kind of time that comes to us from the future. Heidegger explains that 'The counterpart to that dark stillness ['silence' in Stillmark's translation] is the brighter earliness – brighter because it is an even stiller and therefore other childhood'. The last line of 'Jahr' 'calls this stiller childhood the beginning' (1971: 176): 'Goldenes Auge des Anbeginns, dunkle Geduld des Endes' (Trakl 2001: 94). Heidegger sees that the poem heralds 'the arrival of that which has been. This is not what is past, but rather the gathering of essential being, which precedes all arrival in gathering itself into the shelter of what it was earlier, before the given moment' (1971:

176-7); that which Heidegger understands as the 'gathering of essential being', I would call the spirit of poetry, which summons from 'the beginning of the unborn kind':

> The end is here not the sequel and the dying away of the beginning. The end precedes, namely as the end of the decaying kind, the beginning of the unborn kind. Yet the beginning has already overtaken the end as the earlier earliness. [Das Ende ist hier nicht die Folge und das Verklingen des Anbeginns. Das Ende geht, nämlich als das Ende des verwesenden Geschlechtes, dem Anbeginn des ungeborenen Geschlechtes vorauf. Der Anbeginn hat jedoch als die frühere Frühe das Ende schon überholt.] (Adapted from 1971: 176; 2007: 57)

We can think of the end and accomplishment in terms of 'dark patience', 'which bears hidden things toward their truth'. On the other hand, the beginning 'corresponds to a seeing and minding which gleams golden because it is illuminated by "the golden, the true"' (1971: 177). Although Trakl's work seems only to deal in archetypal images, Heidegger sees that his work is 'historical in the highest sense':

> His poetry sings of the destiny which casts mankind in its still withheld nature – that is to say, saves mankind.
>
> Trakl's work sings the song of the soul, 'something strange on the earth,' which is only just about to gain the earth by its wandering, the earth that is the stiller home of the homecoming generation.

At the end of his interpretation of the poet, Heidegger asks,

> Is this dreamy romanticism, at the fringe of the technically-economically oriented world of modern mass existence? Or –

> is it the clear knowledge of the 'madman' who sees and senses other things than the reporters of the latest news who spend themselves chronicling the current happening, whose future is never more than a prolongation of today's events, a future that is forever without the advent of a destiny which concerns man for once at the source of his being? (1971: 196-7)

Some friends of mine would boldly claim with Heidegger that 'Trakl's poetry is not dreamy romanticism: he is a courageous poet-prophet at the darkest moment before the dawn of a new age!' But I have many friends who would exclaim, 'Heidegger is talking utter nonsense. Where are you living, Edward, in cloud-cuckoo-land? Watch the news you old-fashioned Romantic fool!' Perhaps this divided response is indication enough that we live in an age on the cusp of two kinds of time, at the intersection of two cycles, or ways of being, in the Great Year.

Many modern English philosophers would no doubt rebuff Heidegger's resounding words too. Many thinkers today do not see any reason to question what A. W. Moore has called 'the Basic Assumption', 'which involves a cluster of interrelated ideas about the unity, substantiality, and autonomy of reality', and which is expressed as follows: 'representations are representations of what is there anyway' (2000: 74 and 280). In other words, we are subjects surrounded by an objective world.

Blake would have said that such reasoning makes us trapped by cold floods of abstraction. Yeats likewise challenges current common assumptions about reality. Turning away from mere representations, he looks inwards:

> I know now that revelation is from the self, but from that age-long memoried self, that shapes the elaborate shell of the mollusc and the child in the womb, that teaches the birds to make their nest; and that genius is a crisis that joins that buried self for certain moments to our trivial daily mind.

> There are, indeed, personifying spirits that we had best call but Gates and Gate-keepers, because through their dramatic power they bring our souls to crisis[.] (1980: 272)

Yeats's 'Gate-keepers' make us question 'the Basic Assumption', they bring our souls to crisis, so that we are provided with that 'seeing and minding which gleams golden', or 'that Golden Key' as the attendant Spirit in *Comus* calls it, to open 'the Palace of Eternity' within, providing us with more room than any spot of time from past experience. Then, unlike Theseus in *A Midsummer-Night's Dream*, we apprehend more than cool reason ever comprehends. We come to see that everything that lives is holy and that we all exist in the mind of God, which is our friend within, to paraphrase the thirteenth-century Persian poet, Rumi.

The Oxford philosopher Moore and many others today would accuse me of mysticism. They would say that I am suffering from 'the fantasy of the infinite – the desire, especially acute in the Renaissance, to aspire towards the infinite and to be effectively "all there is"' (Reisner 2009: 65-6). But then that must be true, as I hope I demonstrate in this book, of all the great English poets, indeed of all great poets.

All true poetry is mystical. As Robert Graves rightly said, the function of poetry is the same now as it was at the beginning of civilization: it is 'religious invocation of the Muse; its use is the experience of mixed exultation and horror that her presence excites'. Once upon a time the application of poetry was a warning to keep in harmony with the world and its creatures 'by obedience to the wishes of the lady of the house'. Nowadays that house is in disarray: man has disregarded the warning of poetry and 'by capricious experiments in philosophy, science and industry' (1999: 10), which rest on the 'Basic Assumption', we have brought ruin on our family and ourselves.

Poetry can provide each of us with a key to the mansion within, where shadowy things work their changes, so that we return to our world today with the insights of supernatural spirits, which are valuable as long as we appreciate the close relation between truth and fiction, revelation and concealment. When a man would thus know himself through an initial engagement with the art of poetry, his relations with others become stronger and he understands that surrounding objects do not constitute a reality wholly outside of his subjectivity. By reminding us that reason must serve the creative imagination, and that everything natural has a supernatural cause, poetry teaches us that the earth is not a resource to be exploited to the peril of the world and its population. At the same time, and as certain as I am about the great good of poetry, we must remember to treat supernatural beings within poetry with the utmost respect and circumspection: as the Muses warned Hesiod: '"we know how to say many false things similar to genuine ones, but we know, when we wish, how to proclaim true things"'. True poetry is that which loves to conceal, in order ceaselessly to reveal, the truth.

I do think that Wordsworth understood this much by March 1804, when he was looking over earlier material and expanding the poem that became *The Prelude*. At the end of what quickly grew into a new Book V, in lines composed at that time, he pursues his still obscure sense of supernatural forces like the Muses at work in poetry, by wondering about the special influence of books on those brought up in the country:

he, who, in his youth
A wanderer among the woods and fields,
With living Nature hath been intimate,
Not only in that raw unpractis'd time
Is stirr'd to ecstasy, as others are,
By glittering verse; but he doth furthermore,
In measure only dealt out to himself,
Receive enduring touches of deep joy

From the great Nature that exists in works
Of mighty Poets. (*1805 Prelude,* V. 610-9)

The editors of the Norton edition of *The Prelude* explain rather weakly, 'Wordsworth's claim is that a country child will feel a special joy in poetic descriptions of Nature' (Wordsworth 1979b: 184). I feel that something is being said that is greater than this gloss allows. What is 'the great Nature that exists in works | Of mighty Poets'? Wordsworth continues with his own gloss:

Visionary Power
Attends upon the motions of the winds
Embodied in the mystery of words.
There darkness makes abode, and all the host
Of shadowy things do work their changes there,
As in a mansion like their proper home: –
Even forms and substances are circumfus'd
By that transparent veil with light divine;
And through the turnings intricate of Verse
Present themselves as objects recognis'd,
In flashes, and with a glory scarce their own. (*1805 Prelude,* V. 619-29)

What can Wordsworth possibly mean by these lines that retain still their obscurity in subsequent revisions? The 'host | Of shadowy things' sounds like an army of fairies in our fallen world; they are English cousins of the 'host' that rides 'from Knocknarea' in Yeats's 'The Hosing of the Sidhe', '*And if any gaze on our rushing band, | We come between him and the deed of his hand, | We come between him and the hope of his heart*' (1950: 61): such are the kinds of supernatural beings that haunt the first drafts of *The Prelude*.

The 'mansion', which is 'like their proper home', sounds as if it has been sublet from Milton's attendant spirit, 'Before the starry threshold of *Joves* Court', its neoclassical façade concealing one of the 'many mansions' promised by Jesus 'In my Fathers house' (John 14. 2). A mansion can be in a house because, etymologically, it is a place where one stays, a room in which we rest, an apartment, a stopping place on a journey (through 'New Jerusalem', the eternal city, that is 'my Fathers house'). Keats liked to 'compare human life to a large Mansion of Many Apartments', believing Wordsworth's 'Genius' to be 'explorative of those dark passages' that lead from 'the Chamber of Maiden-Thought, which we discover after we have left 'the infant or thoughtless Chamber' (2002: 89-90). A few generations later, in 'A Postcard from the Volcano', Stevens finds the mansion 'shuttered', or shut up, 'A dirty house in a gutted world' that contains 'A spirit storming in blank walls' (1954: 159). Such a mansion can be renovated ceaselessly since it is the site where the supernatural will occur, the event of the poem and the poem itself, 'a happening about to happen' without which the poem cannot happen. A mansion is the magnetic place of supernatural invocation.

All the same, I am still inclined to ask with Jonathan Wordsworth: 'How much effect are the winds really felt to have in Wordsworth's sentence? Where is it that the enigmatic "darkness makes abode" – in winds? or in words?' Jonathan solves some of the mystery by numbering Wordsworth among the 'mighty Poets': a 'cluster of verbal echoes refers us back to... what may well be earliest lines in *The Prelude*' (1984: 224), that is, lines from a fragment composed in February 1798, originally written in the third person because intended for another poem called *The Ruined Cottage*:

there would he stand
Beneath some rock, listening to sounds that are
The ghostly language of the antient earth
Or make their dim abode in distant winds
Thence did he drink the visionary power[.] (1977: 154-5)

In these lines of 1798, the 'ghostly language of the antient earth' is the sacred, otherworldly, and insubstantial language of Nature; it is also the language of ghosts and the tutelary spirits of the countryside. In the lines of 1804, from the end of Book V of *The Prelude*, Wordsworth's concern is instead with our language, with 'the mystery of words in which he had been able to embody his response. In effect, he is saying, visionary power is inherent in the language I then used': as Jonathan Wordsworth understands, 'Wordsworth is seen drawing strength from his own inspired earlier poetry in very much the same way that he draws it from memories of an imaginative childhood'. The poet is expressing 'a new hope that in the uncomprehended workings of language itself there are creative powers' (1984: 225).

By 1804 Wordsworth had come to understand for himself that the genii of folklore, the guardian spirits of his childhood in the Lakes, have taken up their abode in his poetry, just as they had migrated to earlier 'mighty Poets' like Shakespeare and Milton. Wordsworth's poetry has half-provided 'Ye Elves' with a new home. More importantly, within that new home, which is renovated by every sensitive reader's response to the poet's work, they have the chance to cohere: as each reader is transformed by reading Wordsworth's passages, these guardian spirits collect themselves from a state of quaint polytheism into an embodiment of the One Life: the one-in-many and the many-in-one.

Such powers abide in the motions of words, working their changes 'As in a mansion' built up by poet, poem and reader, 'their proper home', the moment of our engagement with language half-arranged by the poet. As Jonathan Wordsworth has argued, 'Veiled… behind the lines of Book V is the border hope that neither [Wordsworth] nor Coleridge ever dared to express that poetry itself, the act of writing, is "a repetition in the finite mind of the eternal act of creation in the infinite I AM" – a repetition that does not always, or merely, co-exist "with the conscious will"' (1984: 226; quoting from Coleridge 1983: 1. 304).

Then the 'shadowy things' become part of the 'moving soul' of Wordsworth's 'long labour' (*1805 Prelude,* XIII. 171 and 172); 'Ye Elves' cohere into 'Wisdom and Spirit of the universe! | Thou Soul that art the Eternity of Thought' (*1805 Prelude,* I. 429-39): more is witnessed in the poetry than 'fancies images', which are merely 'modified by that empirical phenomenon of the will, which we express by the word CHOICE' (Coleridge 1983: 1. 305), and 'growes to something of great constancie', despite our scepticism and ourselves.

Chapter 3

Shakespeare's Seven Acts of Soul

Deep things

I agree with T. S. Eliot that 'Dante and Shakespeare divide the modern world between them; there is no third'. But I take issue with his differentiation of these two towering poets: 'Shakespeare gives the greatest *width* of human passion; Dante the greatest altitude and greatest depth' (1986: 265). In Dante's *Divine Comedy* the pilgrim journeys down to the bottom of Hell, to be turned about, in order to climb through Purgatory to Paradise. Eliot implies that there is no such climbing of the spiritual ladder in Shakespeare: his work is concerned primarily with the affairs of this world. That seems to be the opinion of many critics today. But such a verdict makes Shakespeare reflect merely our age, rather than his own. In fact, as his great rival Ben Jonson well knew, 'He was not of an age, but for all time' (Shakespeare 1953: 1. li)! In this chapter I would like to consider the great altitude and great depth of the lines cast by Shakespeare in the world to prove how his work is also for eternity.

So let's begin at the bottom or rather with Bottom. At the end of act four of *A Midsummer-Night's Dream*, after he has spent most of the play '*with the Asse head*' (III. i. 115) in the company of the Fairy Queen, this swaggering hempen home-spun awakes, transformed back into his original form:

> I have had a most rare vision. I had a dreame, past the wit of man, to say, what dreame it was. Man is but an Asse, if he goe about to expound this dreame. Me-thought I was, there is no man can tell what. Me-thought I was, and me-thought I had. But man is but a patch'd foole, if he will offer to say, what me-thought I had. The eye of man hath not heard, the eare of man

> hath not seen, mans hand is not able to taste, his tongue to conceive, nor his heart to report, what my dreame was. I will get *Peter Quince* to write a ballet of this dreame, it shall be called *Bottomes Dreame*, because it hath no bottome; and I will sing it in the latter end of a play, before the Duke. Peradventure, to make it the more gracious, I shall sing it at her death. (IV. i. 210-28)

When I quote these lines, almost half-way through this book, I think, why should I be such an ass, such a patched fool, to offer any criticism of poetry at all? A professional fool's motley is a better outfit than an academic gown for those who would go about to expound Shakespeare. Why should I bother to explain this endlessly fascinating body of work? Perhaps I would be better off composing the ballad, *Bottom's Dream*. Then again, Bottom's lines might just provide asinine modern criticism with a purpose. Let us remember also that Apuleius' ass was transformed back to Lucius the day after his prayer to the moon, which afforded his vision of the Great Goddess. Perhaps Bottom can lead us by the light of his lines.

I wonder how would Shakespeare's contemporaries have expounded or interpreted his plays? There was no such thing as professional criticism in the late sixteenth century and students and teachers certainly were not writing essays on English literature at that time. But what would Nick Bottom have made of *A Midsummer-Night's Dream* had he been to see the play during the rainy summer of 1596? He is a weaver, but he clearly has some education, since he can read, has some knowledge of classical mythology, and likes to perform plays, sometimes before the Duke and Duchess themselves. He is of the same class as Shakespeare's father who was a glove-maker, and he might well have had ambitions to send a son to university to make him a gentleman. He would probably be living among the aspirant middle classes were he alive today. How would he have expounded the play in the tavern afterwards?

Bottom's comic misremembering of 1 Corinthians – 'The eye of man hath not heard, the eare of man hath not seen, mans hand is not able to taste, his tongue to conceive, nor his heart to report, what my dreame was' – proves that the Bible was never very far away from people's minds in the late sixteenth century, if they were called upon to explain the significance of something, like a play or a dream. And this character is clearly familiar with Tyndale's recent translation, as his very name also indicates:

> But as it is wrytten: The eye hath not sene and the eare hath not hearde nether have entred into the hert of man the thinges which God hath prepared for them that love hym. But God hath opened them unto us by hys sprete. For the sprete searcheth all thynges ye the botome of Goddes secretes. (2009: 1 Corinthians 2. 9-10)

In the 1560 edition of the Geneva Bible, Tyndale's translation is modified, perhaps by propriety, so that 'the botome of Goddes secretes' becomes 'the deepe things of God' (2007), and we can assume that Bottom, like Shakespeare, would also have been familiar with that version of the Bible and its glosses. The headnote to chapter 2 of 1 Corinthians explains that Paul '*putteth for example his maner of preaching, which was according to the tenor of the Gospel. Which Gospel was contemptible and hid to the carnal, And againe honourable and manifest to the spiritual*' (2007). Paul preaches like Christ who spoke in parables: both rely on allegory.

No doubt, as a carnal or natural man, Bottom would have heartily appreciated all the filthy bits of Shakespeare, but he would also have found, almost automatically as a frequent church-goer, more spiritual significance in the plays than many modern theatre-goers. If they catch the allusion at all, most readers today just think that Bottom is being impiously, although perhaps unwittingly, irreverent when he misremembers Paul:

Shakespeare is being audaciously and hilariously blasphemous by renaming the deep things of God, *Bottom's Dream*. I think it is significant that Bottom is called Bottom: Shakespeare's characters move from the depths of the punning potential of that word to its heights, from consideration of one kind of bottom to concern for the deep things of God. Shakespeare's plays explore, like Dante's *Divine Comedy*, the greatest altitude, as well as the greatest depth, of human passion, to put receptive and attentive hearers and readers on a special kind of journey.

Among the carnal, I find critics like Peter Holland, who argues that it is 'dangerously easy to overvalue this "rare vision"' (Shakespeare 2008: 82), and Robert Carver, who asserts that:

> Bottom's famous speech, 'Man is but an ass, if he go about to expound this dream', could almost serve as a motto for Shakespeare's own aesthetic philosophy. Shakespeare's genius (and much of his enduring appeal) is, to an extent, a function of his escape from allegory, his rejection of the exegetical tradition that dominates the Middle Ages and pervades the Renaissance. (2007: 444-5)

Among the spiritual, I find critics like Harold Goddard, who sees that 'what Shakespeare has caught in perfection [in Bottom's waking] is the original miracle of the Imagination, the awakening of spiritual life in the animal man' (1960: 1. 80), and even Harold Bloom, who sees Bottom as a Blakeian 'apocalyptic, unfallen man, whose awakened senses fuse in a synesthetic unity' (1999: 167). HRH The Prince of Wales emphasizes the miraculous quality of Shakespeare's poetry:

> Each of his lines instantly reveals multiple levels of meaning. In his own day they would not just have served those in his audience who were there simply for the action and the

> apparent drama of his plays but also those, like him, who were steeped in the esoteric learning of the Platonic tradition. These people would have discerned the far deeper meaning of his words, recognising, no doubt, what it was in Shakespeare's art 'giving invention light' ...By enchanting us with his poetry, Shakespeare opens our minds to the Divine. (Zinman 2009: 27-9)

Bottom's waking up from his dream or rare vision is part of a series of awakenings at the end of *A Midsummer-Night's Dream*. In Chapter 2 I have already attempted to expound Hippolyta's reaction to the lovers' stories after they have awoken, which itself constitutes a kind of spiritual awakening, and should act as a guide to expounding the play. Ewan Fernie has recently asked, 'if humanity can be recreated on stage, perhaps it can be renovated off stage as well' (2005: 5)? I would affirm that the final awakening in the play is intended to be that of the spiritual life in its reader or audience.

No epilogue is spoken by Bottom when he finally performs his play with Peter Quince and the others before the Duke and Duchess, although one imagines that would not be the time for the ballad of *Bottom's Dream*, and Quince would not have had time to write it in any case. But the tricksy spirit, Robin Goodfellow or Puck, dismisses us with an epilogue, which may well provide opportunity for each of us to attempt *Bottom's Dream* after all:

> If we shadowes have offended
> Thinke but this (and all is mended)
> That you have but slumbred heere,
> While these visions did appeare.
> And this weake and idle theame,
> No more yeelding but a dreame,
> Gentles, doe not reprehend.

If you pardon, we will mend.
And as I am an honest *Pucke,*
If we have unearned lucke,
Now to scape the Serpents tongue,
We will make amends ere long:
Else the *Pucke* a lyar call.
So good night unto you all.
Give me your hands, if we be friends,
And *Robin* shall restore amends. (V. i. 430-45)

When Puck talks of 'the Serpents tongue', he means literally the hissing of a dissatisfied audience, when he would prefer to be given 'your hands', so that we might form a ring of appreciative applause. It is significant that the only real dream in the play involves a serpent. When Hermia wakes from a brief sleep near the beginning of her time in the wood she cries out to her lover who is ignoring her as he exits, following Helena, with whom he has been drugged to fall in love on waking:

Helpe me *Lysander,* helpe me; do thy best
To plucke this crawling serpent from my brest.
Aye me, for pitty; what a dreame was here?
Lysander looke, how I do quake with feare:
Me-thought a serpent eate my heart away,
And you sat smiling at his cruell prey. (II. ii. 145-50)

Dream interpretation in Chaucer's, as well as in Shakespeare's, day relied heavily on Macrobius' classifications in his *Commentary on the Dream of Scipio,* a late classical explication of a dream in Cicero's *On the Commonwealth,* which builds on a now largely lost antique tradition of dream interpretation. Broadly speaking, there were two kinds of dreams: if you had eaten or drunk too much, you would be likely to have an *enhypnion,* a non-predictive and insignificant fantasy that merely reflected some everyday anxiety or desire, such as a nightmare (*insomnium*) or an apparition (*visum*); should you be in a more receptive and temperate state of mind on sleeping, you might be visited by a predictive and highly significant *oneiros*, that is, an enigmatic (*somnium*), prophetic (*visio*), or oracular (*oraculum*) dream. Such dreams may show you directly what will occur or they may deploy allegory to show you indirectly. Such dreams reveal another order of reality; they matter because they come to the dreamer from beyond his fancy (see Macrobius 1952).

We should ask with Hermia, 'what a dreame was here?' Just before she slept, she had to convince her lover to sleep slightly away from her since they are alone at night in a wood. The dramatic situation makes the dream seem to be a mundane *enhypnion*. As Holland says, echoing most readers and audiences today, 'It did not need Freud to identify the serpent of Hermia's dream as a phallic threat... A Freudian reading of the dream would find in the object of the phallic attack, Hermia's breast and heart, a displacement from her vagina' (2008: 13-4). Slightly later in the play, Hermia herself seems unconsciously to consider the dream to be a prophetic *oneiros*, half-remembering the dream to transform it from *somnium* almost to *visio*: when she accuses her lover's rival of her lover's murder, she compares the rival to the serpent of her dream: 'Could not a worme, an Adder do so much' (III. ii. 71)?

How might Shakespeare have interpreted Hermia's dream? I think that he would have identified profound esoteric meaning in the serpent and the heart as well as sexual implications. Hermetic Occult Neoplatonism swept through European intellectual and literary circles through the sixteenth century, as Frances Yates has demonstrated, and Shakespeare's work was influenced by the Neoplatonist theories of Giordano Bruno and John Dee, Queen Elizabeth's mathematician, probably through his patron, the Earl of Southampton, who was great friends with the Earl of Essex, patron to Sir Francis Bacon. It is conceivable, therefore, that

Shakespeare would have had some knowledge of the *Hermetica*, a collection of theological-philosophical texts, which come from late antiquity, but which were believed by Renaissance scholars to be written by Hermes Trismegistus, who was thought to be a contemporary of Moses. In the first part of that book we are presented with a divine *oneiros*, or vision of creation that includes a significant serpent.

Once when thought came to Hermes Trismegistus 'of the things that are' and his 'thinking soared high', his bodily senses were restrained as if he were heavy with sleep, and 'an enormous being completely unbounded in size', calling itself Poimandres, seemed to appear:

> in an instant everything was immediately opened to me. I saw an endless vision in which everything became light – clear and joyful – and in seeing the vision I came to love it. After a little while, darkness arose separately and descended – fearful and gloomy – coiling sinuously so that it looked to me like a [snake]. Then the darkness changed into something of watery nature, indescribably agitated and smoking like a fire; it produced an unspeakable wailing roar. Then an inarticulate cry like the voice of fire came forth from it. But from the light... a holy word mounted upon the [watery] nature, and untempered fire leapt up from the watery nature to the height above. The fire was nimble and piercing and active as well, and because the air was light it followed after spirit and rose up to the fire away from earth and water so that it seemed suspended from the fire. Earth and water stayed behind, mixed with one another, so that [earth] could not be distinguished from water, but they were stirred to hear by the spiritual word that moved upon them. (Copenhaver 2000: 1)

We have happened upon the text that can help us to apprehend the great depth of Shakespeare, deeper even than Dante's Satan at the bottom of Hell: Hermia dreams of primordial matter itself at the heart of her being. How do we find our way back up to Shakespeare's great altitude? How do we turn this dream about? Poimandres explains the vision to Hermes Trismegistus:

> 'I am the light you saw, mind, your god... who existed before the watery nature that appeared out of darkness. The light-giving word who comes from mind is the son of god... that in you which sees and hears is the word of the lord, but your mind is god the father; they are not divided from one another for their union is life.' (Copenhaver 2000: 2)

That which is revealed to Hermes Trismegistus macrocosmically is presented to Hermia microcosmically. Even her name makes her out to be a female counterpart to the supposed author of the *Hermetica*, a reincarnation of the god Hermes, to be identified with the Egyptian god of letters, invention and wisdom, called Thoth. Hermia's dream reveals her to be a kind of unwitting initiate in Hermetic Occult Neoplatonism, yet unable to interpret the vision afforded to her in the wood: 'Aye me, for pitty; what a dreame was here?' When she and Bottom awake, separately and at different moments, each offers a paradigm of different kinds of spiritual awakening that each of us might undergo during and after the play. We might ask Hermia's very question of *A Midsummer-Night's Dream* itself. The play may even be so coded to make us unwitting initiates like Hermia: to afford us such vision from its future as well as make us laugh.

According to Chevalier and Gheerbrant's *Dictionary of Symbols*, the serpent is 'a continuation of the infinite materialization which is none other than primordial formlessness, the storehouse of latency which underlies the manifest world', not so much an archetype, but 'an archetypal complex, linked to the freezing, clammy subterranean darkness of the beginning of things', 'an "Old God", the first god to be found at the start of all cosmogenesis, before religions of the spirit dethroned him' (1996: 845), as Apollo was to kill the python at the beginning of Ovid's *Metamorphoses* (just before he chases Daphne literally into a laurel tree as the lovers will chase each other in the woods outside of Athens after Hermia's dream in *A Midsummer-Night's Dream*):

> Like Ancient Egyptian thought, Greek thought only disapproved of the serpent to the extent that it attempted to reduce the cosmos to its original chaos. On the other hand, to the degree that it remained the essential other side of the spirit, the life-giving force which inspired the sap to rise from the roots to the crown of the tree, it approved and even glorified it. (1996: 850)

To think of the serpent merely as a satanic phallic symbol, without acknowledging its positive properties, is to 'deny primeval life' and 'to deny all the nocturnal properties of which [the serpent] partakes and which are the spirit's clay' (1996: 858). The heart, the other symbol of Hermia's dream, can be understood as 'the centre of every individual's life, will and intellect': 'the heart within us is the symbol of the presence of the godhead and of our awareness of the presence' (1996: 480); the seat of the feeling intellect, 'that intangible point where the created being encounters God', according to Titus Burckhardt (quoted in Chevalier and Gheerbrant 1996: 482). That which Hermes Trismegistus witnesses from without, Hermia experiences within herself, symbolically speaking: the primal act of creation that occurs for all eternity and for each of us every day. Such, I contend, would be the interpretation of Hermia's dream of any Hermetic Occult Neoplatonist attending the play and indeed of Shakespeare himself. The dream is at once an *enhypnion*, revealing the virgin Hermia's fears about sex, but also and more importantly, the highest kind of *oneiros*, repeating the eternal act of creation in the imagination of an unwitting initiate.

In Hermia's dream primordial formlessness in the form of a serpent is devouring spirit in the form of a heart. She is poised to play a cosmic game of snakes and ladders or *Paramapada Sopanam*, which can be conceived as a version of the cabbalistic Tree of Life. Her dream of the snake delivers her to the bottom of the spiritual ladder dreamt of by Jacob in Genesis (28. 10-19), just as the pilgrim at the end of Dante's *Inferno* finds his way up out of Hell by climbing down Satan's body. Since Bottom contains 'the deepe things of God', according to his very name, we might say that he embodies the beginning of the Bible, which records the next stage of Hermes Trismegistus' vision, the next step up the spiritual ladder, when 'the earth was without forme & voyde, and darknes was upon the depe, & the Spirit of God moved upon the waters' (Genesis 1. 2). When Bottom awakes it is also almost on a cosmic scale, as earth and water commingled 'were stirred to hear by the spiritual word that moved upon them' in the vision of Hermes Trismegistus. When we awake from the slumber of watching *A Midsummer-Night's Dream*, nothing less than such stirring might occur: a macrocosm is breaking out of a microcosm as each self is stirred within by the eternal act of creation to create for itself *Bottom's Dream*. Ted Hughes was apt to emphasize Shakespeare's incredible capacity for symbolic language and metaphor (see 1993), and when we expound the symbols of Hermia's dream, we find that we are provided with a key, not only to the play itself, but also to our unimaginable creative potential today.

Puck, or the actor playing Puck, wishes to escape the hissing of the audience's serpent tongue. If we are merely entertained by the play, but do not believe in its magic, do we not also behave like the serpent in Hermia's dream, interpreted at its lowest level of significance as an anxious *enhypnion*? Our earthy scepticism eats the play's heart away, while we sit smiling at our disbelief's cruel prey. If the spiritual life in each of us is stirred by the creative magic of the play, does it uncloak a twofolded, rather than a merely bad, kind of serpent in each of us?

As the Fairy Queen falls sleeps, an attendant fairy sings: '*You spotted Snakes with double tongue, | ... | Come not neere our Fairy Queene*' (II. ii. 9-10). We might think that these spotted creatures are pernicious, like the serpent in Genesis or Demetrius, the rival lover of Hermia, a 'spotted and inconstant man' who speaks with 'doubler tongue' (I. i. 110 and III. ii. 72). Then again, to attempt to speak with a perhaps even doubler tongue, finding spiritual as well as literal meaning in the play as a whole, we see that even spots are not necessarily bad since in the gold coats of cowslips 'spots you see, | Those be Rubies, Fairie favors, | In those freckles, live their savors' (II. i. 11-3), as Wordsworth's 'spots of time' 'retain | A fructifying virtue' (see *1799 Prelude*, I. 288-94), despite my misgivings about them in Chapter 1 of this book.

On the 'banke where the wilde time blowes', where the Fairy Queen sleeps, 'there the snake throwes her enammel'd skinne, | Weed wide enough to rap a Fairy in' (II. i. 249 and 255-6); the serpent, it seems, in such a place, is charmed to do good for others and renew itself. If the snake's skin was spotted, when a fairy wears it as a coat, one imagines those spots transmuted into something beneficent or full of savours, like the smell of Noah's sacrifice to God after the Flood: 'And the Lord smellyd a swete savour and said in hys hert: I will hence forth no more curse the erth for mannes sake for the ymaginacyon of mannes hert is cruell even from the very youth of hym' (2009: Genesis 8). God will no longer sit 'smiling at his cruell prey', lest He become like mankind, the heart of His creation, the home of His spirit on earth, and that which He has almost destroyed in the Flood, its deep waters symbolizing, like the snake, primordial chaos. But we can make reparation for our cruel imaginations through good works, as the gloss to this text in Matthew's Bible indicates: 'The Lord smellyinge of savoure: is the allowance of the workes of the faithfull' (2009). God's example is our best guide to savouring *A*

Midsummer-Night's Dream, and works of faithful imagination bring us closer to God.

Eternal lines

Most among Shakespeare's first audiences would have been uninitiated in Hermetic Occult Neoplatonism, but nearly everyone then would have been adept, or at least reasonably competent, at interpreting texts allegorically, simply from attending church regularly and hearing the Bible expounded there. Medieval traditions of biblical exegesis would have informed their appreciation, and Shakespeare's writing, of vernacular work. Early modern minds were better, more habitually, accommodated than ours to symbols, despite the Reformation. It is to speak merely from within the inhibiting confines of our own still largely materialistic and overly rational, late modern, age to assert that 'Shakespeare's genius… is a function of his escape from allegory'. In fact, his appeal to readers of the future will always depend to no small extent on his acceptance and transmutation of 'the exegetical tradition that dominates the Middle Ages and pervades the Renaissance'. How can Shakespeare's plays awaken the spiritual life today, even if, or especially because, we do not ourselves practice Hermetic Occult Neoplatonism or attend church regularly any more?

Let us begin to respond to Shakespeare as his contemporaries would, that is, as Dante advised we read his *Divine Comedy*, and we will find an old system of interpretation is reborn for modern purposes. The fourfold method of interpreting Dante's poem is explained in the Epistle to Can Grande by making reference to the Psalm that is sung by souls in the boat to Purgatory – 'When Israel went out of Egypt, the house of Jacob from a people of strange language' (Psalms 114. 1):

> if we consider the letter alone, the thing signified to us is the going out of the children of Israel from Egypt in the time of

> Moses; if the allegory, our redemption through Christ is signified; if the moral sense, the conversion of the soul from the sorrow and misery of sin to a state of grace is signified; if the anagogical, the passing of the sanctified soul from the bondage of the corruption of this world to the liberty of everlasting glory is signified. (Dante 1920: 199)

Such an interpretation builds on Thomas Aquinas' way of reading the Bible. He sees that book in a twofold light, making a distinction between its literal sense and its spiritual sense, which 'is based on and presupposes the literal sense' (Aquinas 1964: 1. 39). When Aquinas divides the spiritual sense into three, he refines his definitions in relation to time: out of its literal meaning in everyday or historical time, the reader of scripture discovers the allegorical or typological sense, which connects the Old Testament with the New, the moral or tropological sense, which allows us to apply the Bible to our lives today, and the anagogical sense, which is eschatological, that is, to do with eternal things to come. According to this fourfold method of interpretation, by one act of reading we might realize two or four kinds of time, but anagogy does not apprehend us without our first comprehending the text's literal meaning, its historical truth.

Aquinas justifies the polysemantic nature of the Bible by drawing attention to its divine authority. In the *Divine Comedy* Dante makes 'the allegory of the poets [...] (a metaphorical narrative sense)' serve 'an allegory of the theologians (a true ultimate literal or historical/theological sense, all metaphors stripped away)'. Poetic fictions that make use of metaphors as well as 'figural allegory, in which the literal sense was historically true' can possess fourfold meaning. 'The pilgrim's journey' in the *Divine Comedy* is 'a system of metaphors for the process by which a living man, on earth, comes to understand the nature of the cosmos and the state of souls after death' (Dante 1996-2011: 3. 9-10). Can Shakespeare's body of work enable its creator and future readers to journey to such knowledge in order to remake our soul on earth?

That carnal critic Carver asks, 'Even if we "take a chance", as Tobin urges us, in adopting an allegorical approach, what is our reward' (2007: 445)? Recently, Ira Zinman and Margaret Healy, critics I would number among the spiritual, have offered impressive interpretations of Shakespeare's sonnets that draw on medieval methods of biblical exegesis. As Zinman has asserted, 'In his plays and Sonnets, Shakespeare was able to write simultaneously on the levels of literal meaning as well as the allegorical, moral, and anagogical meanings' (2009: 40). Healy also sees that 'In Shakespeare's hands poetic making – the major preoccupation of the [sonnets] – cannot be disentangled from soul remaking and divine considerations'. For her, 'The central sonnets of the sequence reward consideration from this perspective' (2011: 179). Ted Hughes, in his monumental and largely underestimated late work, *Shakespeare and the Goddess of Complete Being*, has discovered for our modern age the anagogical significance of the whole of Shakespeare, by outlining a Mythical Equation that gives rise to the major plays and includes Christianity.

The Prince of Wales rightly draws attention to the instantaneity of multiple levels of meaning in Shakespeare's lines. The carnal and the spiritual are both right in their interpretations of Shakespeare; and both wrong, if either denies the validity of the others' interpretations. The miraculous thing about Shakespeare's work is that it can mean opposite things at once. His texts are oxymoronic from beginning to end and in that way they foreshadow, not only the destabilization campaigns of postmodernism, but Blake's insight that 'Man has no Body distinct from his Soul for that calld Body is a portion of Soul discernd by the five Senses. the chief inlets of Soul in this age' (*The Marriage of Heaven and Hell*, Plate 4).

Before interpreting the plays to find their anagogical significance today, we can turn to the *Sonnets*, a sequence of poems whose special private circumstances of composition allowed Shakespeare freer play of his esoteric learning than in the theatre. These poems, which are often concerned with their own survival into future generations of readers, were also eventually published for wider public consumption; they do not so much presuppose as speculate about any future reader's competence in unfolding hidden depths of their meaning.

Literally speaking, it seems that the most powerful man in England at the time, Lord Burghley, had employed Shakespeare to write some poems to persuade his ward, Henry Wriothesley, the aforementioned Earl of Southampton, to marry. Others conjecture that it was in fact the Countess of Pembroke, dedicatee of Sir Philip Sidney's *Old Arcadia,* who had commissioned the first seventeen or so of the *Sonnets,* for her son, William Herbert, Earl of Pembroke. No doubt we will never know for sure the genesis of the sequence or the true identity of the addressee.

In any case, most readers of the *Sonnets* feel that Shakespeare falls in love with the young man between sonnets 17 and 18, and then the sequence takes on a life of its own, as the poet stops trying to persuade the young man to marry, and delineates instead their love affair, until the twelve-line poem that is numbered 126 in the sequence. From sonnet 127 to sonnet 152 the focus shifts to a dark lady. The final two are elaborations on a Greek epigram. These poems were first published in 1609 as a Quarto with another related poem, 'A Lover's Complaint', appended. Many were written in the 1590s, when there was a vogue for writing sequences of sonnets; a few may date from the 1580s, and there is much internal evidence to suggest that Shakespeare was still writing fresh sonnets, and revising old ones, to compile the sequence through the early 1600s.

I believe that Shakespeare ordered the poems into a sequence himself since the numbering of sonnets seems particularly pertinent to their meaning and many together form mini-sequences within the collection as a whole. In fact we can read numbers 15 to 19 as such a mini-sequence in order to discern the latent spiritual significance of the *Sonnets*, giving their invention light. I find the literal circumstances of the *Sonnets*, the poet's love affairs with a mysterious young man and a dark lady, central to the sequence in the same way that Rumi's love for the mysterious, even disreputable, Shams-e Tabrizi (the sun of Tabrizi) compels his beautiful collection of poems, the *Divan-e Shams-e Tabrizi* (see 2001). I am also happy to find that Hughes believes 'that Sufi link might not be so fanciful' (1993: 61). In different ways, these poets find in mysterious earthly figures the Divine Beloved.

One of the themes of this chapter is interpretation itself because I see that Shakespeare at once repels and attracts commentary. Enormous attention has already been paid to the *Sonnets* through the generations. Mostly critics have focused on the literal meaning of the poems, becoming intrigued, for example, by the identity of the characters in the unfolding drama. Few have attempted to discern any spiritual significance. But sonnets 15 to 19 might just anticipate this very situation in which the deeper meaning, the bottom of the poems' secrets, hides in plain sight from an uncomprehending future audience.

The division that most commentators discern in the sequence as a whole between sonnets 17 and 18 is encompassed by the mini-sequence from 15 to 19. Among modern critics only a very few, like Zinman, believe 'the theme' of this group to be 'man's spiritual renewal' (2009: 209). In sonnet 15, all the world's a stage:

When I consider every thing that growes
Holds in perfection but a little moment.
That this huge stage presenteth nought but showes
Whereon the Stars in secret influence comment.
When I perceive that men as plants increase,
Cheared and checkt even by the self-same skie:
Vaunt in their youthful sap, at height decrease,

And were their brave state out of memory.
Then the conceit of this inconstant stay,
Sets you most rich in youth before my sight,
Where wastfull time debateth with decay
To change your day of youth to sullied night,
And all in war with Time for love of you
As he takes from you, I ingraft you new.

Katherine Duncan-Jones's indispensible edition of the *Sonnets* exemplifies the modern approach to interpreting these poems. Here is how she sums up the theme of 15: 'Viewing the instability of all mortal things... the poet sees that youth, too, is subject to age and decay. He attempts to renew his friend's beauty by means of verbal wit' (Shakespeare 2010: 140). It's hard to argue with that. But it is surely a reading firmly entrenched in literal sense, as is made clear when we turn to Zinman's summary of the poem's theme, which focuses on its spiritual significance: 'One life is a short span compared to all eternity, and it is a stage upon which the cosmic Director plays the drama of life and death. Mankind would be lost but for the Love of God which ever showers His children with grace, and keeps them ever hopeful and renewed' (2009: 177-8). I believe that the poem is designed to sustain both of these kinds of readings.

Often very clever modern critics, like John Kerrigan in his edition, will assert quite nonchalantly, 'Shakespeare, of course, was not a neoplatonist' (Shakespeare 1999: 52), Kerrigan's 'of course' and use of the lower-case 'n' signifying, presumably, his disapproval of Neoplatonism. Others will tell you otherwise. In his reading of the spiritual significance of sonnet 15, Zinman substitutes God for the human lover, just as Sufi poetry transmutes the conventions of love poetry to talk about the divine friend within. Is this too easy a swap for modern readers? You may think so, but even the unRomantic Kerrigan must acknowledge the height of this range of meaning in the sequence:

> it seems highly significant... that Shakespeare should think of his friend in violently reversed metaphors, subduing the nature of things for the sake of his beloved's particularity and being... The beloved becomes, in other words, not the world's tenor but its grand and elusive vehicle. In poetry, after all, the logically distant term frees language into suggestion; images lend resonance to their ground... and Shakespeare lets his subject resound... until he writes a kind of pantheism... the youth is made a kind of god. (Shakespeare 1999: 30-1)

It seems that both Stevens and Shakespeare 'say God and the imagination are one' (1954: 524). In the *Sonnets* the friend of the poet is at once human and divine. The poems sustain simultaneously literal and spiritual interpretations, and neither kind of interpretation is valid without the other. What Aquinas says of the Bible is true of our other Bible, Shakespeare's *Complete Works*: its spiritual sense 'is based on and presupposes the literal sense'. The word 'presupposes' here translates the Latin word 'supponit', from *suppono*, to put, place, or set under. The spiritual sense is founded on literal sense but it also puts that sense in its place: ultimately we must understand that the spiritual sense has always come before, despite what we perceive to be its literal foundations.

Suppono can also mean particularly to substitute one person or thing for another, and that is just what is happening in Shakespeare's *Sonnets*. In sonnet 15, in particular, the poet is 'all in war with Time for love of you', just as the spiritual meaning of the poem is in war with its exegetical future in time, and that which cannot be expressed must be at odds with the very words of the poem. The divine friend within would substitute for the human friend without; the poem's highest or anagogical sense would subject its literal meaning in time. Obeying this divine impulse, which emerges in the process of making the poem itself, the poet finds that he is in war with time, eternity breaking out in language that is also subject to time. The literal meaning of the poem is that which time takes from God, until we only recognise the 'you' of the poem as a human lover subject to time, but the poem, in carefully organized lines of language, ingrafts God continually again in each human involved in its making: lover, poet and reader.

In sonnet 15 the poet contemplates the inevitable decay of all kinds of natural things, but he comes to understand, during the process of making the poem, that the soul grows stronger as the body gets older, as long as 'I ingraft you new': as long as each makes his soul in God, acknowledging that art has a part to play in that making. Etymologically, grafting a scion to a stock is related to writing; 'ingraft' is derived ultimately from the Greek word for stylus or pencil: as the *OED* says, 'the transferred sense of "scion, graft" was suggested by the similarity of shape'. Shakespeare's pen, cut like a scion, will cause the young man to flourish or fructify as God in the future, ingrafting itself on the page. Throughout this mini-sequence Shakespeare builds on the image of scoring lines, sometimes competing with time that makes wrinkles on any face, thus 'I ingraft you new' also suggests engraving and makes the poem a kind of epitaph on a tomb, a meaning offset by sexual innuendo also to be found in the expression.

From the bottom of such latent significance, taking the poem from God with time, 'I ingraft you new': I substitute the eternal for you; anagogy, which comes to us from the future, from what is always new, is now growing out of, by substituting itself for, the poem's literal sense in the future. Duncan-Jones notices 'an ingenious pun' in the last lines of 15: 'The poet engages in a continuous process of writing, or engraving, so that the repeated "you" sounds... are converted, by the addition of an 'n' into the sound *new*. The effect is of a word-game, in which time's removal of *-th* from *youth*, leaving a bare *you*, is outsmarted by the poet's conversion of the word into *new*' (Shakespeare 2010: 140). As a scion grows out of the stock, so God grows anew out of you, that is, addressee, future readers and poet as reader of the emergent sense of his work. You may think that I am making the word 'new' do too much work here, but this 'word-game' is reminiscent of cabalistic 'techniques for manipulating the letters of the Hebrew alphabet for purposes of mystical contemplation': for example, 'the S in the Name of Jesus makes audible the ineffable Name (composed only of vowel sounds) and signifies the Incarnation, the Word made flesh or made audible' (Yates 2001: 3 and 23). Can it be the case that the addition of 'n' to 'you' renews the youth as God in you? As the thirteenth letter of Shakespeare's alphabet, 'n' evokes Christ celebrating the Last Supper or Zeus sitting among the twelve Olympians.

Zinman says of the end of 15: 'As an observer and expounder of truth, the Poet does in fact bring a message of hope and redemption to help men on the stage of life play their parts in a more divine way' (2009: 182). I would like to explore the ways in which only poetry can 'bring a message' to help us to climb up from the stage of the world to different stages of existence.

After the first sixteen or seventeen procreation sonnets, as Hughes has pointed out, Shakespeare 'never mentions begetting heirs again... Instead he offers his poetry alone as the sole perpetuator, to all succeeding generations, of the young man's beauty, worth and truth, as if these sonnets were some altogether superior kind, some divine, immortal kind, perhaps, of female reproductive system' (1993: 54). In fact, this transformation has already occurred in sonnet 15, except sonnet 16 begins with a 'But', making it a sequel poem, reverting to the belief that 'The penis, mightier than the word, replaces' (Shakespeare 1999: 194) 'this (Times pensel or my pupill pen)': begetting heirs is 'a mightier waie' of defying time than making art. The very sequence of poems is in labour, a kind of primordial labour that makes its own womb, transforming itself, in its contractions, into something that can give birth to apprehensions previously latent in our consciousness. As it becomes a divine female reproductive system, the miraculous womb of the 'Goddess of Complete Being', Shakespeare's collection of sonnets might benefit from the midwifery of criticism, the maieutic productivity of explication that can unfold the poems' spiritual message: that we are greater than we know, the divine force, to be delivered from the poems, already inside each reader, including the poet, who must find himself continually catching up to that which is disclosed by his emergent work.

Sonnet 17 is ostensibly the last of the procreation sonnets, but this contraction of meaning is full of latent significance:

> Who will beleeve my verse in time to come
> If it were fild with your most high deserts?
> Though yet heaven knowes it is but as a tombe
> Which hides your life, and shewes not halfe your parts:
> If I could write the beauty of your eyes,
> And in fresh numbers number all your graces,
> The age to come would say this Poet lies,
> Such heavenly touches nere toucht earthly faces.
> So should my papers (yellowed with their age)
> Be scorn'd, like old men of lesse truth then tongue,
> And your true rights be termed a Poets rage,
> And stretched miter of an Antique song.
> But were some childe of yours alive that time,
> You should live twise in it, and in my rime.

As the idea of the lover's future child becomes in the next sonnet that sonnet itself, so the lover becomes God in any interpretation that would find spiritual meaning in the sequence. And I would argue that Shakespeare himself interprets his own sonnets, within the sonnets, in this manner. Trakl's vision of 'Golden eye of inception, dark patience of the end' (2001: 95) unfolds the same process, and Heidegger's explication is again pertinent:

'The end is here not the sequel and the dying away of the beginning. The end precedes, namely as the end of the decaying kind, the beginning of the unborn kind. Yet the beginning has already overtaken the end as the earlier earliness' (Adapted from 1971: 176). Between sonnets 15 and 19 we find ourselves at the end of the decaying kind in the process of preceding the beginning of the unborn kind.

In the eighteenth century, Samuel Johnson could discern well the end of the decaying kind reflected in Shakespeare's *Complete Works*. Echoing Hamlet's theories about 'the purpose of Playing' (*Hamlet*, III. ii. 23), he says that 'Shakespeare is above all writers, at least above all modern writers, the poet of nature; the poet that holds up to his readers a faithful mirror of manners and life' (2000: 421). By the beginning of the nineteenth century, Coleridge, believing in the power within Shakespeare's verse, discerned there the beginning of the unborn kind, and he felt compelled to say:

> Shakespeare, no mere child of nature; no automaton of genius; no passive vehicle of inspiration possessed by the spirit, not possessing it; first studied patiently, meditated deeply, understood minutely, till knowledge become habitual and intuitive wedded itself to his habitual feelings, and at length gave birth to that stupendous power, by which he stands alone, with no equal or second in his own class[.] (1983: 2. 26-7)

We are also among those who will read 'my verse in time to come', and it may be said that many of us do not 'beleeve' it any more. Many modern readers are closer to Johnson than Coleridge in outlook, and would want to summarize 17 as follows: 'living descendants of the addressee will demonstrate to future ages the truth of the claims made for him by the poet' (Shakespeare 2010: 144), and leave it at that. Would Shakespeare's original coterie of readers, well versed in esoteric philosophy, have thought such a summary too sceptical about the poem's spiritual latency? The poem indirectly directs us to move beyond Duncan-Jones's superficially literal interpretation. Zinman's more spiritual-minded summary of 17 may be after all more faithful to the verse, and closer to the ways in which the poem was interpreted by its intended audience: 'Spiritual truths are often not readily apparent in scriptures or verse. Uncovering the deeper meaning requires a heightened awareness, which is itself a sign of spiritual growth' (2009: 196-7): reading Shakespeare, as well as the Bible, can help you to make your soul. Is Shakespeare declaring, by not declaring, 'my poems conceal a hidden meaning from the future'? Is the poet suggesting that any future reader will be born again if she apprehends the bottom of the poem's secrets in her heart?

If we substitute God for human lover, then 'some child of yours' alive in the future is not a particular descendant, but each of us as a future reader of that poem, already unconsciously attuned to God. In the next sonnet, that very poem substitutes for the addressee's future descendant: it is implied in this transition from 17 to 18 that Shakespeare's verse itself has a part to play in awakening God in the imagination of future readers. Even if we do not consciously acknowledge this process, and you may violently disagree with my suggested manner of interpreting the *Sonnets*, it will occur regardless each time the verse is read, because in each case the lines allow the more than human element in language to speak from the future, from behind the masks of poet, lover and future reader.

As we have already seen Rilke admit, that which is more than human enters humans as the future itself, emblem of God in time, just as the thirteenth letter, 'n', is at once extraneous (at least to the first twelve letters) but now central (at least according to the future of Shakespeare's alphabet), and can signify, in this twofolded way, Christ among the apostles: 'We cannot say who has come, perhaps we shall never know, but there are many indications that it is the future that enters into us like this, in order to be transformed within us, long before it actually occurs' (2011: 52). Shakespeare's sonnets are in labour to give birth to their anagogical sense, such significance preceding their composition, but also dependent on the future that transforms itself and the poems by helping to unfold them. 'You should live twise in it, and in my rime': the comma after 'it' in the original 1609 edition of the sonnets serves to emphasize that word (see Shakespeare 2012: 142). According to the poem's literal significance the 'it' refers to a future descendant of the addressee. There are different nuances of meaning: you would live two successive times, your own life repeated in that of your descendant, as well as a third time in 'my rime'; or you would live again twice, your image recreated by your offspring and in my poems. If the 'it' also refers to any future reader who believes the verse, that is, who reads the poem for its spiritual significance, then, as Zinman interprets, 'the Lord will be awakened in their hearts, and in the Sonnets' (2009: 200), because those future readers who believe will also make the addressee live again as God reborn in themselves.

The fact is that most readers today do not believe in the sonnets as Zinman does. But our very incomprehension of the poems from their future is dramatized in this mini-sequence from 15 to 19 as the ostensible subject matter changes by expansion and contraction from procreation to poetry. The poems have two kinds of future: in the interpretation and the poems of future readers and in God. Reading the sonnets today, we are in the same situation as the prisoners in Prospero's '*Line-grove*' (*The Tempest*, V. i. 10), which is presumably a stand of lime trees or lindens, but also Shakespeare's verse, as long as we understand Prospero, speaking in this instance, to stand for God:

Their understanding
Begins to swell, and the approaching tide
Will shortly fill the reasonable shore

That now ly foule, and muddy: not one of them
That yet lookes on me, or would know me[.] (V. i. 79-83)

Our very incomprehension is part of the process of the Divine coming into play from the future on earth today and in these poems, one kind of future substituting for another in time: and we should know that truth loves to conceal itself so that it may be ceaselessly unconcealable. In these sonnets we are witnessing the labour of our potentiality: something that was hidden is being delivered from the future, but that very process involves our incomprehension, our continual happening upon that self greater than we can know as we read. If we knew it all already then each poem would fail to make us apprehend that we are greater than we know. And we will never know it all already. The 'reasonable shore' is always shortly to be filled.

The very movement of the lines in Shakespeare's *Sonnets* dramatizes this process of the freshest truth only revealing itself in the most furtive fiction: that which expands is in love with its contractions. Meaning changes dramatically as you read from word to word and from line to line, a subsequent line changing the meaning of the one before it. The very beginning of 15 at once demonstrates and articulates this way that meaning grows in verse: 'When I consider every thing that growes | Holds in perfection but a little moment.' When we turn from the first to the second lines, we realize that the first line lacks a 'that' after 'consider': the poet is not after all considering everything that grows, that is, all life on earth, but the fact that all life inevitably decays; that 'perfection' of meaning of the first line is held only as long as it stands alone, 'but a little moment', before the second line delimits the all-encompassing vision to a meditation on transience. Then again, that 'little moment' is also made by the verse to hold in perfection the vision of every thing that grows: such a reading of the poem, industrious to find its latent meaning, finds 'a moment' that 'renovates' all those other moments of decay. The poem turns out also to be one of the 'Auguries of Innocence', 'To see a World in a Grain of Sand | And a Heaven in a Wild Flower | Hold Infinity in the palm of your hand | And eternity in an hour' (Blake 2008: 490).

Sonnet 18 expands on this kind of growing:

Shall I compare thee to a Summers day
Thou art more lovely and more temperate:
Rough windes do shake that darling buds of Maie,
And Sommers lease hath all too short a date:
Sometime too hot the eye of heaven shines,
And often is his gold complexion dimm'd,
And every faire from faire some-time declines,
By chance, or natures changing course untrimm'd:
But thy eternall Sommer shall not fade,
Nor loose possession of that faire thou ow'st,
Nor shall death brag thou wandr'st in his shade,
When in eternall lines to time thou grow'st,
So long as men can breath or eyes can see,
So long lives this, and this gives life to thee,

Note the comma at the end of this poem, in its original printing; the number '18' also has a period point, unlike the other numbers in the sequence. These are errors of the typesetter no doubt, but such slips perhaps reveal something of the anxiety of giving birth in verse as well as in life: sometimes we stumble across the threshold as unwittingly as the compositor arranging letters that he did not compose himself.

Line 12 causes me the most trouble in this famous sonnet. Stephen Booth argues: 'a reader may well understand *lines* in its root meaning, "cords" or "ropes," and take *in eternal lines* as "bound eternally." That reading is sustained – though finally made less ominous – by *to time thou grow'st,* which recurs to the grafting metaphor of 15.14... a graft is usually bound in place by cords until it has coalesced with the stock'. He also thinks that 'lines' 'suggests "lines of life," the threads spun by the Fates in classical mythology' (Shakespeare 1978: 162). Colin Burrow summarizes in a slightly different but related manner: 'The addressee of the poem is like a shoot grafted into time's substance, and continues to live through either the poet's *lines* or his own *bloodline*' (Shakespeare 2002: 416). Such simultaneity of meaning presupposes the addressee to be at once human and divine: the poetry is in labour to make each addressee (future readers as well as original 'begetter') 'live twise', not so much a second time, physical likeness memorialized in descendants and verse, but in a twofold degree, finding spiritual significance in life and poetry.

By the end of sonnet 19, poetry has completely taken the place of future children as a means of defying time, an ancient but familiar personage: 'Yet doe thy worst ould Time dispight thy wrong, I My love shall in my verse ever live young'. In later sonnets, like 53, the conflation of God and the young man is unavoidable: 'What is your substance, whereof are you made, I That millions of strange shadowes on you tend?' Such a sonnet troubles Kerrigan: 'The "master-mistress" of Sonnet 20 becomes the cynosure of all loveliness, not only male and female but past as well as present, mythic as well as real... But if the young man is a god... why does he tread "on the ground" [130. 12]' (Shakespeare 1999: 31)? The answer is: because the poet is addressing the divine potential of any human; the sonnets would awaken that 'bright eternal Self' (Yeats and Swami 1970: 135) that lives at once in poet, addressee and future readers on earth. It is implied that the writing and reading of poetry have central parts to play in that process. By marrying 'A gentler Sien [Scion], to the wildest Stocke', Shakespeare's art ('That Nature makes' along with 'knowledge become habitual and intuitive'), makes 'conceyve a barke of baser kinde I By bud of Nobler race' (see *The Winter's Tale*, IV. iv. 86-97): as He wishes, God is ingrafted into man by such twofold art as Shakespeare's.

Stage by stage

The poet of sonnets 15 to 19 has melancholic tendencies: in other words, he is at the first stage of spiritual development; he is at the beginning of the soul-making path that ends in apprehension of that 'bright eternal Self' that lives within man. In fact, the first conceit of sonnet 15, that this world is a 'huge stage', echoes the most famous speech of the second most famous melancholic in Shakespeare, Jaques in *As You Like It*. Duke Senior, exiled in the Forest of Arden, has just sent off Orlando to fetch his weak companion, 'an old poore man', oppressed with age and hunger. The Duke takes a kind of comfort in their afflictions: 'This wide and universall Theater: | Presents more Wofull Pageants then the Sceane | Wherein we play in', prompting the melancholy Jaques to say:

> All the world's a stage,
> And all the men and women, meerely Players;
> They have their *Exits* and their Entrances,
> And one man in his time playes many parts,
> His Acts being seven ages. At first the Infant,
> Mewling, and puking in the Nurses armes:
> Then, the whining Schoole-boy with his Satchell
> And shining morning face, creeping like snaile
> Unwillingly to schoole. And then the Lover,
> Sighing like Furnace, with a wofull ballad
> Made to his Mistresse eye-brow. Then, a Soldier,
> Full of strange oaths, and bearded like the Pard,
> Jelous in honor, sodaine, and quicke in quarrell,
> Seeking the bubble Reputation
> Even in the Canons mouth: And then the Justice
> In faire round belly, with good Capon lin'd,
> With eyes severe, and beard of formall cut,
> Full of wise sawes, and moderne instances,
> And so he playes his part. The sixt age shifts

Into the leane and slipper'd Pantaloone,
With spectacles on nose, and pouch on side,
His youthfull hose well sav'd, a world too wide,
For his shrunke shanke, and his bigge manly voice,
Turning againe toward childish treble pipes,
And whistles in his sound. Last Scene of all,
That ends this strange eventfull historie,
Is second childishness, and meere oblivion,
Sans teeth, sans eyes, sans taste, sans every thing.
Enter Orlando with Adam. (II. vii. 129-66)

Jaques describes the seven ages of man in this world. Jonathan Bate has recently organized his 'intellectual biography' of Shakespeare around this famous speech, using each of the seven ages as an invitation 'to consider a cultural moment and a broad theme' (2009: 4). We should also know that the number seven has spiritual significance. God's creation of the world lasts seven days, if we include his rest on the seventh, and each of our weeks is an invitation to incorporate that process during our own lives. Augustine divided biblical history into six ages, reflecting the seven days of creation, and illustrating mankind's journey to find eternal rest in God. The seven liberal arts of the medieval curriculum are so organized to help understanding proceed upwards to be replenished in God.

Many religions think of man's spiritual ascent as occurring over seven steps. For example, the Shaman will undertake a seven-step ecstatic journey 'through the celestial regions', indicated by 'The identification of the seven-branched Cosmic Tree with the seven planetary heavens' (Eliade 2004: 275 and 274). It helps me to think about such journeying as a process of seven rites of initiation in which one of the seven virtues or 'angels' helps us to overcome one of the deadly sins, each personified as a 'demon': when we are on the spiritual path, Wrath, Greed, Lust, Sloth, Envy, Gluttony, and Pride can be transformed into Peace, Generosity, Purity of Intent, Courage, Compassion, Temperance, and Humility. We proceed from knowledge of our personalities and physical selves, eventually to leave that self behind, discovering a profounder self in God. Shakespeare's major plays dramatize characters undertaking, or failing to undertake, such a spiritual journey during the course of their plays.

Jaques' speech describes different stages of a very secular life, but its mundanity is put in place by its dramatic context: the speech is delivered to Duke Senior, symbol of God in man, as Orlando goes off to fetch old Adam. The very names of these characters lend their resonance to Jaques' almost cynical appraisal of a life. 'Adam' in Arden recalls our first parent in Eden, our journey through life, as it is described by Jaques, very different from Adam's existence before he was expelled from that golden land, a descriptor suggested by 'Orlando': or-land. You could also say that during this speech that recounts any man's life, our original self, Adam, is carried O'er-land-0: that is, over ground zero, Orlando signifying at once the golden land and our world, to find God within. Jaques' seven-step worldly life, which was caused by Adam's transgression in Eden, can be transformed in the theatre – a wooden kind of zero in Shakespeare's day – so that we learn to travel through it to where we already are: 'sans every thing' but close to God. The soul is reminded on this journey, in the face of God, that it is nothing, 'just as the Arabic word for "nothing" is virtually the same as the Hebrew name for the first man: '*adam*' (Upton 2008: 56): attending to Shakespeare, we find ourselves, not so much on Jacob's, but Jaques', ladder, the hidden *axis mundi* that grows through *The Complete Works*.

Why is Jaques called Jaques? His name reaches from the bottom to the heights of significance. The etymon of Jaques is 'jakes', a privy. The name was, literally speaking, a joke for Shakespeare and his contemporaries. It is also the first syllable of 'Shakespeare': 'By identifying himself in this role as Jaques,

Shakespeare converts his own name into a transitive phase' (Hughes 1993: 102). The name also recalls St Jaques and thus the Epistle of James in the New Testament in which faith is closely associated with good works; in the words of the headnote to the 1560 edition of the Geneva Bible, James exhorts us 'to declare a true faith by livelie frutes... and to bring him which is out of the way, to the knowledge of Christ': 'What availeth it, my brethren, thogh a man saith he hathe faith, when he hathe no workes? can the faith save him' (2007: James 2. 14)?

As much as Shakespeare's plays entertain us by dramatizing man's seven ages in this world, I believe that they also perform good works: Shakespeare's plays are intended to be lively fruits of faith, bringing readers and audiences to spiritual knowledge. Jaques' speech is a kind of purgation of soul on earth so that Shakespeare can make his work into a soul-making ladder, or tree on which to grow such fruits of life as can make good our purloined fruits of knowledge. As Healy has boldly argued:

> The artist-philosopher had first to cleanse his soul in order to let in more heavenly light and thus recapture traces of divinity lying tarnished within himself if he wanted to progress and reach the dizzying innovative heights of 'alter deity'. He had to rekindle the Sun/Son within himself: it was Christ's incarnation that made possible the restoration of humanity to its prelapsarian state.

Importantly, 'Writing poetry – doing art – is integral to soul remaking, to mending inner nature' (2011: 178-9 and 182), and that is just the kind of work that Shakespeare's *Complete Works* performs for spectators and readers as well as for the writer.

Jaques is a melancholy man; he has a temperament that encompasses what is high and low. Among the four humours, according to the Galenic classification that 'locked man's psychology into the cosmos', melancholy was often considered to be the 'most unfortunate and the most hateful'. Sanguine people were active and hopeful men of affairs; choleric people were quick in quarrel; phlegmatic people inclined to lethargy; but melancholics were often 'sad, poor, unsuccessful, condemned to the most servile and despised occupations'. By the Renaissance, however, the theories of Pseudo-Aristotle had been assimilated by Neoplatonists to revalue melancholy, raising it from the lowest to the highest of the humours. It was thought 'that the heroic frenzy, or madness, or *furor*, [the 'Poets rage' of sonnet 17], which according to Plato is the source of all inspiration, when combined with the black bile of the melancholy temperament produces great men; it is the temperament of genius': by Shakespeare's day melancholy had become the humour of 'great thinkers, prophets and religious seers' (see Yates 2001: 59-61), and so it is entirely appropriate that Jaques should be predominantly of that humour as a type of the spiritual pilgrim or initiate (who even intends to join the 'Religious life' of 'convertites' where 'There is much matter to be heard, and learn'd', at the end of *As You Like It*: V. v. 188 and 190-1). As such Jaques prefigures the most melancholy of all of Shakespeare's characters: Hamlet.

Yates has already formulated the major question to be asked of Hamlet: is his 'a good melancholy of inspired vision or a bad melancholy of witchcraft and evil?' Her conclusion is that his 'black humour' is not of Hell, 'but the melancholy of a prophet in a world so badly disobedient to the Law that the universal harmony is inaudible, or broken' (2001: 181). Angels, like Devils, work through the agency of a melancholic man's heightened imagination. In the previous chapter we have seen Wordsworth, as he begins *The Prelude,* becoming possessed, if not quite by devils, at least by lesser tutelary spirits of nature, rather than by higher Neoplatonic angels. Hamlet, then, is himself a prototype of the inspired poet in the later modern world. His very imagination or fantasy is at stake. As Healy says:

> angels when minded to inspire man to prophecy, can only work through the physiological manipulation of the imagination. We should recall how Sidney's *Apology* celebrates the relation between poetry and prophecy. Used correctly, the fantasy is thus truly wondrous. However, because it relies on the input from external sight, smell, touch, taste and hearing it can be easily contaminated by the body's drives and excesses; additionally, bad spirits and the devil access the imagination in the same manner as good spirits and angels – fantasy is thus an intensely ambivalent power around 1600. (2011: 185)

Hamlet, like an Hermetic Occult Neoplatonist, strives for heightened vision, his aim is to purge and so organize his mind that the soul's eye sees 'more truly' (Stevens 1954: 65) and clearly. *Hamlet* is a play about the painfulness of that process of becoming disillusioned and less attached to material things, including the very theatre in which we watch him speak.

After his father's ghost has spoken to him, Hamlet seems resolved to revenge his murder:

> Remember thee?
> I, thou poore Ghost, while memory holds a seate
> In this distracted Globe: Remember thee?
> Yea from the Table of my Memory,
> Ile wipe away all triviall fond Records,
> All sawes of Bookes, all formes, all pressures past,
> That youth and observation copied there;
> And thy commandment all alone shall live
> Within the Booke and Volume of my Braine,
> Unmixt with baser matter[.] (I. v. 95-104

Drawn by the ghost from his companions to the heights of the battlements of Elsinore, Hamlet has had a covenant moment with the ghost of his father. In fact, Shakespeare draws heavily on Moses receiving the ten commandments from Yahweh on Sinai as a template for this scene (see Exodus 19-34 and Fisch 1999: 86-7): we are invited by such imitation and echoing of the Bible to substitute God, Christ, or Jesus the Imagination, for Hamlet's father's ghost (probably played by Shakespeare himself when it was first performed at the Globe Theatre in 1600). Hamlet receives a single commandment, reminding us that Christ's one commandment in John supersedes and encompasses the ten given to Moses: 'that ye love one another, as I have loved you' (15. 12).

A twofold reading of Hamlet's lines, taking the hint from Shakespeare's use of Christ's repeated exhortations to the disciples to 'remember' as he gives his commandment in John (15. 20 and 16. 4), as well as the Sinai episode in Exodus, understands that the character is at once talking of the ghost's commandment to kill and Christ's commandment to love others. The play's drama unfolds between its literal and spiritual senses. *Hamlet* is made out of its protagonist's profound spiritual concerns, a path initiated, ironically, by an injunction to kill. Since we are all born 'astride of a grave' (Beckett 1990: 83), such is the situation of any soul that would make itself in this world: doomed to death we must forget ourselves and love one another to find God disconcertingly nearby.

The way in which Hamlet describes the workings of his memory shows that he is acquainted with classical and Renaissance memory systems so essential to the work of soul-making for Hermetic Occult Neoplatonists. In fact, he refers to two interrelated models: the seal-in-wax model of cognition and the architectural mnemonic or places-and-images memory scheme.

According to Socrates each of our souls has been given, by 'Memory, the mother of the Muses', 'a block of wax':

> We make impressions upon this of everything we wish to remember among the things we have seen or heard or thought of ourselves; we hold the wax under our perceptions and thoughts and take a stamp from them, in the way in which we take the imprints of signet rings. Whatever is impressed upon the wax we remember and know so long as the images remain in the wax; whatever is obliterated or cannot be impressed, we forget and do not know. (1997: 212; *Theaetetus* 191d-e)

Mary Carruthers explains that 'the metaphor of the seal-in-wax or written tablets was a model for the process of making the memorial phantasm and storing it in a place in the memory': 'The second major metaphor used in ancient and medieval times for the educated memory... that of *thesaurus*, "storage-room," "treasury," and "strongbox"... refers both to the contents of such a memory and to its internal organization' (2008: 37). Hamlet's mind, his 'distracted Globe', is a storehouse or memory theatre, as Richard Burbage, the first actor to play Hamlet, would have visualized the inside of the Globe itself, while remembering the lines of his part, arranging images for words in its separate bays. The Globe theatre, as its name indicates, is a microcosm of the world itself, but when we venture from the macrocosm of our world to its microcosm, we find that we are transformed, re-imagined by Hamlet, as we sit seated in this storehouse of his very mind (see Yates 2012: 330-54). Each of us is a microcosm of the world: watching *Hamlet* we apprehend simultaneously two kinds of theatres, each inside and outside of ourselves and the world, in order to move from one stage of life to another. Hamlet's triple pun on globe strangely draws attention to his status as a character in a play while simultaneously affirming his reality for the world without and as a model for each audience member to follow within. All the world's a stage, and so conceived, such a stage presents us with a series of stages:

Hamlet's theatre or book becomes a ladder of the soul up which each may climb to find that we are greater than we knew.

Macbeth's melancholic humour is darker than Hamlet's: witches rather than a prophetic ghost have schooled his susceptible imagination. Since bad spirits have had access to his fantasy he ends up despairing:

> To morrow, and to morrow, and to morrow,
> Creepes in this petty pace from day to day,
> To the last Syllable of Recorded time:
> And all our yesterdayes, have lighted Fooles
> The way to dusty death. Out, out, breefe Candle,
> Life's but a walking Shadow, a poore Player,
> That struts and frets his houre upon the Stage,
> And then is heard no more. It is a Tale
> Told by an Ideot, full of sound and fury
> Signifying nothing. (*Macbeth,* V. v. 19-28)

It is surprising how many modern productions of Shakespeare, as well as critical works, make his plays out to be tales told by an idiot, signifying nothing. In *Macbeth,* Shakespeare presents us with the dark side of our world today. Is it possible to find another stage as we strut and fret on the one that Macbeth presents to us? Yates has argued that in this play, 'The magic is bad, an evil necromancy. A few escape from this black night of Hell... but there are no good fairies' (2001: 182). As I have said before, it is my belief that we live in Macbeth's castle today. How can we number ourselves among the few that escape from this Hell that we have invented for ourselves?

Not 'Yesterday, today, and tomorrow', the first two words forcing upon us repeatedly reversed feet and a jarring spondee, but 'To morrow, and to morrow, and to morrow', the very rhythm of the regular iambic pentameter emphasizing '...mor[e] ...and ...mor[e] ...and ...mor[e]', the line's final extra syllable, echoing our sigh of despair or cry at painful life extending itself beyond expectations: as Fintan O'Toole has argued, 'The witches give [Macbeth] a little taste of the future and it becomes addictive', painfully so. O'Toole sees that Shakespeare progressively breaks down 'the whole notion of what is internal and what is external' in *Macbeth*, even more so than in *Hamlet* when we find ourselves sitting on occasion as memory or the world in the protagonist's very mind. Finally, 'Surrounded by his soldiers and his battle flags, Macbeth gives expression to his deepest internal feelings' (2002: 157 and 162) about his wife's death and 'To morrow', and we, who come to the play from its future, are not permitted to distance ourselves from its doomed protagonist:

> His vision of humanity may come out of his personal situation, it may be bleak, but the humanity which he speaks of is still a common humanity. And there is no longer the possibility of deceit. The heart can now be read in the face, the mind's construction emerges directly in the spoken word... For at least one moment in time, a man's inner self is not denied and refuted by the external world of history... It is a moment that cannot last... If we are glad to see Macbeth go, we are also glad to have had that moment. (2002: 162)

I quote O'Toole because that seems to me to be an articulate expression of how most of us would expound the play today: Macbeth's vision is of a humanity that we share with him across the generations, despite extraneous historical circumstances. I take the opposite view: Macbeth's vision of humanity is common because it is historical; we seem to share it at our bleakest moments only because Macbeth perceives clearly our age as a later development of his own, at the end of the decaying kind. Anyone alive must now find himself at the end of that kind of time, before the beginning of the unborn kind. Fittingly, Macbeth is afforded a vision of the unborn kind just before he dies. In fact, he is finally killed off by Macduff who is technically unborn since he 'was from his Mothers womb | Untimely ript' (V. viii. 15-6). Only then, 'the time is free' (V. viii. 55). Our contemplation from the future of Macbeth, attended by his servant Seyton, may well provide the beginning of our way out of Hell on earth today, just as Satan himself is the way out of Hell for the pilgrim and his guide in Dante's *Inferno*. But it is a mistake to think that 'the mind's construction emerges directly in the spoken word': that is to fall into what Blake calls 'Single vision & Newtons sleep' (2008: 722).

His vision of the unborn kind of time came perhaps too late for the finally defiant Macbeth, if not for us. In *King Lear*, written just before *Macbeth*, in about 1605, the protagonist does move from one kind of stage to another. After giving away his kingdom and banishing his youngest daughter, her two sisters betrayed King Lear, and he finds himself out at night on a heath. His attendants, the fool and the disguised Kent, enter a hovel to shelter from a storm, but the King remains on stage to pray:

> Poore naked wretches, where so ere you are
> That bide the pelting of this pitilesse storme,
> How shall your House-lesse heads, and unfed sides,
> Your lop'd, and window'd raggednesse defend you
> From seasons such as these? O I have tane
> Too little care of this: Take Physicke, Pompe,
> Expose thyself to feele what wretches feele,
> That thou maist shake the superflux to them,
> And shew the Heavens more just. (III. ii. 28-36)

After King Lear gives thought to the poor, he understands that 'Pompe', a personification of 'magnificent display of any kind' (Shakespeare 2004: 273), should take purgative medicine, or 'Physicke', in order to pass down, or 'shake', its 'superflux' to the poor. The word 'shake' evokes 'jaques' or a privy and makes any reader wonder what Shakespeare can mean by the word 'superflux', his own coinage, according to the *OED*, which defines it as 'An unnecessary or excess amount of something; a surplus', although R. A. Foakes sees the word as 'disconcertingly hinting at "flux" or discharge from the bowels' (Shakespeare 2004: 273).

From the great depth of his despair, King Lear turns himself about to find the road to spiritual wisdom. Such shaking down of pomp finds for us the spiritual path upward, just as exactly half-way through Canto 34 of Dante's *Inferno*, the pilgrim's descent on Satan's body is pulled by Virgil into an ascent through a cavern to Purgatory:

> When we came to where the thigh is hinged, exactly at the widest of the hips, my leader, with labour and difficulty,
> turned his head to where he had his shanks, and clung to the pelt like one who climbs, so that I supposed we were returning into Hell again.
> 'Hold fast, for by such stairs,' said my master, panting like one weary, 'must we depart from so much evil.'
> Next he went forth through the hole in the rock, and placed me sitting on the rim; then he extended his careful step to me.
> I raised my eyes, thinking to see Lucifer as I had left him, and I saw that he extended his leg upward;
> and if I laboured in thought then, let the gross people ponder it who do not see what point it was that I had passed. (76-93)

I will not be so gross as to dwell on that turning point, but just point out that it is there in Shakespeare too, at the end of the decaying kind, which means that his work can rise just as high as Dante's, apprehending the beginning of the unborn kind. For King Lear at last does take, intermittently forgetting his way, the road to spiritual enlightenment.

King Lear's insight is well articulated by Shantideva's eighth-century didactic poem *The Way of the Bodhisattva*, which focuses on the cultivation and enhancement of bodhichitta. I would go so far as to suggest that Shakespeare's major phase of plays should function in our society as such an exposition of spiritual truths: although presented in the form of entertainment, rather than as Shantideva's style of 'personal meditation', they are 'offered in friendship to whoever might be interested' in spiritual salvation. As recent translators of Shantideva's poem have explained, '*Chitta* means "mind", "thought", "attitude". *Bodhi* means "enlightenment", "awakening", and is cognate with the term *buddha* itself'. Bodhichitta means, therefore, '"mind of enlightenment", "awakened mind" – the attitude of mind that tends towards Buddhahood, the enlightened state'. There are two aspects of bodhichitta: 'ultimate bodhichitta', referring to direct apprehension of 'the true status of phenomena. This is the wisdom of emptiness: an immediate, nondual insight that transcends conceptualization', or the 'nothing' with which King Lear must come to terms. 'Second, there is relative bodhichitta, by which is meant the aspiration to attain the highest good, or Buddhahood, for the sake of all, together with all the practical steps necessary to achieve this goal' (2006: 1, 2 and 3), those steps of which King Lear realizes too late that he has, along with the poor, 'tane | Too little care'.

We can think of one state as 'the wisdom of emptiness' and the other as 'the will to deliver beings from suffering', and although the connection between the two may not be immediately apparent, we can say at this stage that 'The true realization of emptiness is impossible without the practice of perfect compassion, while no compassion can ever be perfect without the realization of the wisdom of emptiness'. This relationship, which perhaps seems impossible at first, is based upon the assertion that the mind or soul itself, even caught up in the endless cycle of death and rebirth to which life in the material world is bound, 'is never, and has never been, ultimately alienated from the state of enlightenment. Bodhichitta is in fact its true nature and condition' (2006: 3).

The 'wisdom of emptiness', at the end of anyone's spiritual path, is also expressed in chapter 11 of the *Tao Te Ching*, which repeats the equivalent of 'nothing' as emphatically as *King Lear*:

> When thirty spokes converge upon the hub
> We make a wheel that owes its use to nothing;
> Wet clay is turned into a bowl and baked
> To make a bowl that owes its use to nothing;
> By putting in some windows and a door
> We build a house that owes its use to nothing:
> Our making use of things depends upon
> Recognizing the benefit of nothing. (see Lau 2001: 14-7; my translation)

I can also see a connection between Christ's commandment in John – 'that ye love one another, as I have loved you' (15. 12) – and 'the will to deliver beings from suffering' so central to Shantideva's poem:

> Those desiring speedily to be
> A refuge for themselves and others
> Should make the interchange of 'I' and 'other,'
> And thus embrace a sacred mystery.

* * *

> All the joy the world contains
> Has come through wishing happiness for others.
> All the misery the world contains
> Has come through wanting pleasure for oneself. (8. 120 and 129)

Macbeth's actions demonstrate how the world's misery comes through wanting pleasure for oneself. King Lear articulates in prayer his desire speedily to be a refuge for others; he does not yet understand that this is the way to 'embrace a sacred mystery', although he comes close, reunited all too briefly with his banished daughter, near the end of the play:

> When thou dost aske me blessing, Ile kneele downe
> And aske of thee forgivenesse: So wee'l live,
> And pray, and sing, and tell old tales, and laugh

* * *

> And take upon's the mystery of things,
> As if we were Gods spies[.] (V. iii. 10-7)

In *The Tempest*, written around 1611, five or six years after *Macbeth* and *King Lear*, characters are reminded of the mystery of things already apprehended but sometimes forgotten. As Yates has argued, Prospero 'is the climax of the long spiritual struggle in which Shakespeare and his contemporaries had been engaged' (2001: 188). We have seen already in Chapter 2 how it is necessary for the protagonist to renounce his 'rough Magicke' (V. i. 50) in order to advance to 'the next degree of the mage's enlightenment' (Shakespeare 1987: 115). Finally, to embrace a sacred mystery, Prospero must remember his common humanity, not a bored despair about the future, but a willingness to forgive the deceiver, making the interchange of 'I' and 'other', during the precious remainder of a life.

The Tempest is the first play of Shakespeare's first collected works, the *First Folio* of 1623, but it is his final non-collaborative work. Steven Marx has wisely commented, 'I doubt that Shakespeare intended to marry his book to the Bible, as did Dante, Spenser, Milton, and Blake, but I do think he intended them to embrace' (2000: 18), and the first and last chapters of Marx's book on Shakespeare and the Bible discuss *The Tempest*'s relation to Genesis and Revelation respectively. I believe that the play commands such a dual comparison because its anagogical significance is a dramatization of the God of the first book of the Old Testament becoming mankind after the last book of the New Testament.

All of the concerns of this chapter – the dreaming and waking in *A Midsummer-Night's Dream*, the divine reproductive system of the sonnets, and the spiritual ladder that stretches through the plays from *As You Like It* to *The Tempest* – demonstrate Shakespeare's abiding concern with 'that conflict into which Christianity inevitably leads', that burden under which we still groan: '*God wanted to become man, and still wants to*' (Jung 1984: 153). The very positioning of *The Tempest* at the beginning of the *First Folio* is an invitation to find such anagogical sense in Shakespeare's *Complete Works*: such an explication of the play apprehends how there's a divinity already folded around our ends, rough hew them how we will.

Since this chapter is rising to an apocalyptic climax, when 'The trend is towards giving the literal sense a fuller content' (Aquinas 1963: 1. 141) in criticism today, allow me to turn to Jung's late work, *Answer to Job*, in which a primarily anagogical interpretation of the Bible is ventured. But please do not think that makes me a Jungian: I see that the poets of our canon are way ahead of any insights in late modern psychology. Jung is useful to my argument because he also saw, and had the courage to write, near the end of his life, that 'The Book of Revelation rightly placed at the end of the New Testament, reaches beyond it into a future that is all too palpably close with its apocalyptic terrors' (1984: 147). Not content merely to describe the end of the decaying kind, like our current, historically inclined, criticism, Jung would contemplate the beginning of the unborn kind: 'Everything now depends on man: immense power of destruction is given into his hand, and the question is whether he can resist the will to use it, and can temper his will with the spirit of love and wisdom' (1984: 161). Such is the question around which *The Tempest* turns until Prospero is reminded by Ariel of his 'humane' affections and to be 'kindlier moved' (see V. i. 16-24): to put 'kind' back into mankind and become properly human, that is, humane.

The play would have us rise to such a kind of human of the future:

> Since the Apocalypse we now know again that God is not only to be loved, but also to be feared. He fills us with evil as well as with good, otherwise he would not need to be feared; and because he wants to become man, the uniting of his antinomy must take place in man. This involves man in a new responsibility... He must know something of God's nature and of metaphysical processes if he is to understand himself and thereby achieve gnosis of the Divine. (1984: 163-4)

The 'purpose of Playing' is not just 'to hold as 'twer the Mirrour up to Nature' to show 'the very Age and Bodie of the Time, his forme and pressure' (see *Hamlet*, III. ii. 23-7), at the end of the decaying kind, but, as Hamlet also knew, the play is 'the thing, | Wherein Ile catch the Conscience of the King' (II. ii. 633-4), that is, the king within, at the beginning of the unborn kind of time: the play can help each of us to find a way of catching, by not catching, that eternal self or stupendous power that would live in the same house as our everyday selves.

Shakespeare's *Complete Works* has a part to play in man's new responsibility to know something of the Divine that works within him. The different kinds of dreaming in *A Midsummer-Night's Dream*, along with the awakening of the spiritual man in Bottom and potentially each audience member, demonstrate that Shakespeare has already been afforded Jung's insight:

> It is only through the psyche that we can establish that God acts upon us, but we are unable to distinguish whether these actions emanate from God or from the unconscious. We cannot tell whether God and the unconscious are two different entities. Both are border-line concepts for transcendental contents. (1984: 177)

The archetypes, which the serpent of Hermia's dream encompasses, are not 'mere objects of the mind, but are also autonomous factors, i.e., living subjects, the differentiation of consciousness can be understood as the effect of the intervention of transcendentally conditioned dynamisms'. Then again, 'the archetypes cannot be investigated at all without the interaction of the observing consciousness' (1984: 179). Shakespeare understood before Jung that 'There then arises that reciprocal action between two relatively autonomous factors which compels us, when describing and explaining the processes, to present sometimes the one and sometimes the other factor as the acting subject, even when God becomes man' (1984: 180). This kind of reciprocal action arises in Prospero and is, in turn, reciprocated in the reader that would substitute God for that character, such an explication of the play causing the reader to understand that God wants to live in man.

At the end of the play, regretting his decision to rebel against Prospero and subject himself to a jester and a drunken butler, Caliban muses:

> Ile be wise hereafter,
> And seeke for grace: what a thrice double Asse
> Was I to take this drunkard for a god?
> And worship this dull foole? (V. i. 293-6)

No doubt, 'Man is but an Asse', or 'a patch'd foole', 'if he goe about to expound' this play, but I will continue with my folly, and like 'a thrice double Asse', take Prospero, not just for

Shakespeare, as most seem to do, but for a god. At least I am comforted by Marx taking him for the God of Genesis: 'God and Prospero both offer those who successfully pass their qualifying tests – the selected or "chosen" ones – a vision of the future with a promise of fertility and prosperity as a reward for distinguishing themselves from those who are rejected' (2000: 29). Prospero rewards Ferdinand, that other log carrier of the play, with his daughter's hand in marriage, but the following lines should also be read as if God is speaking through Shakespeare to His divine potential in future readers:

> If I have too austerely punish'd you,
> Your compensation makes amends, for I
> Have given you here, a third of mine own life,
> Or that for which I live: who, once againe
> I tender to thy hand: All thy vexations
> Were but my trials of thy love, and thou
> Hast strangely stood the test: here, afore heaven
> I ratifie this my rich gift[.] (IV. i. 1-8)

As Marx expounds, 'Prospero apologizes for his severe treatment of Ferdinand and offers compensation... The gift is his daughter, but also the division of deliverance, fertility, and prosperity in the masque, linked by a rainbow to Jacob's ladder and Noah's flood' (2000: 29). *The Tempest* is a ratification of the rich gift of the divinely inspired *Complete Works of Shakespeare.*

As even the sceptical Theseus knew, 'The Poets eye in a fine frenzy rolling, doth glance | From heaven to earth, from earth to heaven' (*A Midsummer-Night's Dream,* V. i. 12-3): Shakespeare's gift, if we choose to take it, is to put us on, in our world, if not quite Jacob's, then at least Jaques' or Shakespeare's, ladder to God, his inspired work possessing fourfold meaning, and your spiritual potential making its highest sense. That said, we should remember with Jung that:

> even the enlightened person remains what he is, and is never more than his own limited ego before the One who dwells in him, whose form has no knowable boundaries, who encompasses him on all sides, fathomless as the abysms of the earth and vast as the sky. (1984: 180)

A Midsummer-Night's Dream is contrived not only to make us laugh, but to wake us up each time that we see or read the play, to help deliver that with which the sonnets are pregnant: the unknowable or bottomless 'One' that already lives in man. *The Tempest* is at the end of all that art can do for any man on such a spiritual journey to his future in God, that is, human apprehension of divine imagination. When we begin to read Shakespeare's *Complete Works* from its end in *The Tempest*, like Prospero, 'Every third thought shall be my grave' (V. i. 311), and we find that what is of the highest spiritual significance there gives each receptive man's life its creative meaning, especially in the world today.

Chapter 4

The Poet as Avatar

Milton, melancholy and the meaning of Urania

In his early twenties, Milton resolved to become '*Il Penseroso*', and, as that pensive or thoughtful man, he chooses to live with the lady '*Melancholy*', a 'Goddes, sage and holy' who manifests herself as a 'pensive Nun, devout and pure, | Sober, stedfast, and demure'. It is implied that she also lets herself be heard in the strains of the nightingale's night song or reveals herself as 'the wandring Moon', as if she is an aspect of the Great Goddess herself; and when the weather does not permit *Il Penseroso*'s night walks to commune with her outside, she will preside over his day-dreaming by the fire at home or his studies within his remote hill-top tower of symbolic significance:

> Or let my Lamp at midnight hour,
> Be seen in som high lonely Towr,
> Where I may oft out-watch the *Bear*,
> With thrice great *Hermes*, or unsphear
> The spirit of *Plato* to unfold
> What Worlds, or what vast Regions hold
> The immortal mind that hath forsook
> Her mansion in this fleshly nook:
> And of those *Dæmons* that are found
> In fire, air, flood, or under ground,
> Whose power hath a true consent
> With Planet, or with Element. (2009: 53-8)

Murray W. Bundy once half-cautioned that 'Anyone familiar with the vast literature of melancholy from Bright to Burton is likely to understand Mr. Babb when he shares Burton's dismay as he sets out "to adventure through the midst of these perplexities"' (1952: 276). Bundy was reviewing Lawrence Babb's book, *The Elizabethan Malady* (1951), and referring also to Timothie Bright and Richard Burton, two Renaissance scholars who composed a treatise (1586) and an anatomy (1621), respectively, on melancholy. In my experience the study of melancholia induces melancholia, and having touched lightly on the subject in the previous chapter, we will not dwell on it here. I have just given you the necessary references should you wish to enter that complicated labyrinth of dark research. But beware, you might find yourself registering for a PhD that you will probably never submit.

Let me just say that *Il Penseroso*'s kind of melancholy is involved in his pursuit of Hermetic Occult Neoplatonism; he hopes that his meditative temperament will be transmuted by the *furor* of inspiration, allowing the studious poet eventually to 'attain | To somthing like Prophetic strain' (2009: 58). By living with the lady *Melancholy* as an inspired man, the future poet-prophet trusts that hermetic 'knowledge' will 'become... intuitive' and 'wedded... to his habitual feelings', so that he can at length give 'birth to that stupendous power' (Coleridge 1983: 2. 27), which we witness from the future as something greater than Milton understood consciously in *Paradise Lost*, as well as that which sets Shakespeare apart from all other writers. *Il Penseroso* is endeavouring to follow the advice of the Florentine Neoplatonist, Marsilio Ficino, and not the example of Macbeth or even Hamlet, 'to keep his melancholy happily tempered' (Babb 1940: 263).

Il Penseroso is a figure on Jaques' ladder, to use an expression I coined in the previous chapter of this book to describe the soul-making capability of Shakespeare's *Complete Works*: *Il Penseroso*'s previous reincarnations are Shakespeare's great tragic heroes and his future reincarnations are the great poets of English literature. As Milton's ideal self, he is one incarnation of the immortal soul of our national poetry as it journeys through its several lives in this world. It is a crucial incarnation, at once summation and prototype, essentializing the spiritual wisdom of Shakespeare's protagonists, for later poets to follow.

That last paragraph came to me in a flash last night, and my more rational early morning self was about to delete it, when I realized that I am just describing *Il Penseroso* there in his own terms. As an exemplary Neoplatonist, he must believe in metempsychosis, or the transmigration of the immortal soul from life to life. As Milton's ideal poet-scholar, he devotes his studies to the strong Pythagorean element in Plato, which was emphasized by prominent followers such as Plotinus. Inevitably, and reassuringly, I find that Coleridge, another pensive Neoplatonist or reincarnation of *Il Penseroso*, was there before me, with a fitting exclamation:

> O! few have there been among critics, who have followed with the eye of the imagination the imperishable yet ever wandering spirit of poetry through its various metempsychoses, and consequent metamorphoses; – or who have rejoiced in the light of clear perception at beholding with each new birth, with each rare *avatar*, the human race frame to itself a new body, by assimilating materials of nourishment out of its new circumstances, and work for itself new organs of power appropriate to the new sphere of its motion and activity! (1849: 1. 31-2).

That is to say, the work of the greatest English poets carries that burden under which we still groan: '*God wanted to become man, and still wants to*' (Jung 1984: 153). That which Shakespeare delivers from the Bible, with the help of his esoteric studies, during the course of his *Complete Works*, allowing its transmigration from play to play, its continual death and rebirth as the end of the decaying kind precedes the beginning of the unborn kind of time, likewise journeys from work to work, or from *avatar* to *avatar*, through the generations of English poets after Shakespeare. If critics learn to follow that 'wandering spirit of poetry through its various metempsychoses' with 'the eye of the imagination', then they will learn that it is also within them, for 'We say God and the imagination are one' (Stevens 1954: 524).

In his astute review of my last book, Tim Morris complained that my 'intense piety before the poem' can 'tip into a kind of spiritual literalism which should have been checked' (2013: 639): for example, he did not like that I took seriously the 'spirits' who dictated *A Vision* to Yeats, which I will confront once more in the final chapter of this book. And now again, I find my 'intense piety' before Milton's poem tipping into that same kind of 'spiritual literalism'. But I will persist in what many critical contemporaries will see as folly because the older poetry calls for it (such is my piety).

When Milton as *Il Penseroso* declares that he will 'oft out-watch the *Bear*', that is, frequently stay up all night under the constellation of Ursa Major, which never sets, 'With thrice great *Hermes*', I believe that he means, literally, 'in the company of the spirit of Hermes Trismegistus', the supposed author of the *Hermetica*. From the time of the ancient Greeks to Shakespeare's day, 'thrice great *Hermes*' was identified with 'The Egyptian God, Thoth, the scribe of the gods and the divinity of wisdom' (Yates 2002: 2), and it is with such a half-divine, almost mythical, figure that *Il Penseroso* intends to converse. 'Since Ficino's time, Renaissance thinkers had made Hermes a contemporary of Moses and the wellspring of *prisca theologia*, a tradition of gentile theology concurrent with and confirming biblical revelation' (Copenhaver 2000: 1), and 'Il Penseroso' can be read as also engaging directly, literally speaking, with this tradition.

Then again, those disinclined to tip into my kind of spiritual literalism might be surprised that Milton refers to Hermes Trismegistus at all. By the time that 'Il Penseroso' was composed, as Milton would have well known, Isaac Casaubon had questioned the ancient quality of the *Hermetica,* detecting 'biblical, Jewish and Christian language and ideas, thus anticipating the findings of such modern experts as C. H. Dodd', and making 'a strong and dramatic case for "Pseudomercurius" as the figment of a half-Christian forger' (Copenhaver 2000: 1).

So, the ancient authority of the *Hermetica* had been debunked by 1614, the 'thrice great *Hermes*' disparagingly retitled 'Pseudomercurius', and yet, fifteen or so years later, Milton is still invoking that author as a spirit with which to stay up all night. What is Milton playing at? What kind of study is keeping *Il Penseroso* from his bed? We will have to admit that the inspired wisdom of the poem 'Il Penseroso', shared with the figure of *Il Penseroso,* has very little do with the decorum of contemporary academic research. Milton's model of scholarship for the poet is intuitive rather than strictly empirical. *Il Penseroso* will either sit with the spirit of Hermes Trismegistus or quite literally 'unsphear | The spirit of *Plato*' and 'And of those *Dæmons* that are found | In fire, air, flood, or under ground', the same in kind to those we have already encountered in Chapter 2 of this book. The future poet-prophet is not just reading the *Hermetica* and books by Plato: his study of these texts is such that the spirit of these writers is invoked for a more direct kind of communication. You might of course say that Milton is using metaphors to describe intense study. But the poem invites us to take these metaphors seriously, in the manner of all the great poets who come after Milton.

We should know that, as a practitioner of Hermetic Occult Neoplatonism, *Il Penseroso* would have been 'mounting the ladder'. As another one of his reincarnations, Ted Hughes, explains, he would have been 'locking his meditation into overdrive (the *furor* of Love) by various procedures of ritual magic (that would now be called techniques of self-hypnosis)'. He would have been striving 'to open "the black diamond doors" of the psyche, releasing visions, revelations of divine understanding, and even supernatural intelligences and powers' (1993: 22).

Milton is not just being deliberately quaint by ignoring the cutting-edge scholarship of Casaubon; he is calling into question the validity of that kind of historical research when it comes to understanding texts that deal with *prisca theologia* or perennial wisdom. Such texts as the *Hermetica* and Plato's *Dialogues*, as well as Milton's 'Il Penseroso' itself, require not only literal or historical criticism but interpretation that is prepared to rise to the heights of anagogy, and converse with the spirits of their dead authors. Such indeed is the very teaching of those works that cannot be understood properly until we put reason in its useful but subservient place; and current literary criticism, ushered in by such figures as Casaubon, is all too often inhibited by its entirely valid but ultimately narrow positivist and historicist tendencies. *Il Penseroso*'s method of study should serve as a model for literary critics of the future as well as for poets.

'Il Penseroso', the sequel to 'L'Allegro', or the cheerful man, was composed possibly in the early 1630s. Later, during England's Interregnum, the republican Milton devoted most of his time to the mundane affairs of writing prose polemics and public office, half-ignoring his earlier intentions to live in a removed place with *Melancholy*. After he became totally blind in 1652, it is probable that he started to turn to poetry more and more, his 'Soul more bent | To serve therewith my Maker, and present | My true account, least he returning chide' (2009: 304). In 1667 Milton first published his epic poem, *Paradise Lost*, much of it written after the restoration of King Charles II to the throne, when the poet was sometimes in hiding, on the run for his republican activities. The third invocation of *Paradise Lost*, at the opening of Book 7, movingly describes these horribly melancholic circumstances of the poem's composition, while calling down *Urania*, his heavenly Muse, who is also in many ways a magnification or transmutation of lady *Melancholy* in 'Il Penseroso':

> Descend from Heav'n *Urania*, by that name
> If rightly thou art call'd, whose Voice divine
> Following, above th' *Olympian* Hill I soare,
> Above the flight of *Pegasean* wing.
> The meaning, not the Name I call: for thou
> Nor of the Muses nine, nor on the top
> Of old *Olympus* dwell'st, but Heav'nlie borne,
> Before the Hills appeerd, or Fountain flow'd,
> Thou with Eternal Wisdom didst converse,
> Wisdom thy Sister, and with her didst play
> In presence of th' Almightie Father, pleas'd
> With thy Celestial Song. (VII. 1-12)

Urania is the 'ancient Muse of Astronomy', although in the sixteenth century, 'the divine poetry movement reassigned her name to the Christian Muse' (Milton 1998: 388); the meaning of her name makes her 'the Heavenly One' to which Milton calls. In Proverbs 8, Wisdom recounts her activities before Creation:

> The Lord possessed me in the beginning of his way, before the works of old. I was set up from everlasting, from the beginning, or ever the earth was. When there were no fountaines abounding with water. Before the mountains were settled: before the hilles, was I brought foorth. (8. 22-25)

Milton is clearly making an allusion to this text, calling on readers to recall the voice of Wisdom who now cries 'in the top of high places, by the way in the places of the pathes. She cryeth at the gates, at the entrie of the citie, at the comming in at the doores' (8. 1-3), exhorting us in our world today with her memories of her time with God before Creation: 'Then I was by him, as one brought up with him: and I was daily his delight, rejoycing always before him' (8. 30). As Barbara Lewalski explains, 'Milton devises a myth in which that "Wisdom" which is a personification of God's wisdom is the "Sister" of Urania as the Muse of divine poetry ("Celestial Song"); therefore, Urania also originates from God' (Milton 2007b: 175).

The wisdom of poems is quite literally older than the hills, according to Milton. That vagabond or 'ever wandering spirit of poetry', which I would trace in this chapter 'through its various metempsychoses' (see Coleridge 1849: 1. 31-2), is no less than an aspect of 'the Spirit of God' that 'mooved upon the face of the waters' (Genesis 1. 2), and that which cries to us today, neglected like a beggar, at the gates of our cities and at the doors to our homes. This book is intended to help us listen to the wisdom of this 'marginal art form' (Wroe 2006). Milton continues his invocation, acknowledging how he has been up led by this heavenly Muse to tell of battles in Heaven and the fall of Satan and his armies to Hell before the Creation of man. Now he needs the Muse to descend to earth to help him relate the Creation and Fall of man and his Expulsion from Eden, the episodes that make up the remainder of the poem, the dreary circumstances of the poet's own broken life sadly a part of that very story:

Up led by thee
Into the Heav'n of Heav'ns I have presum'd,
An Earthlie Guest, and drawn Empyreal Aire,
Thy tempring; with like safetie guided down
Return me to my Native Element:
Least from this flying Steed unrein'd, (as once
Bellerophon, though from a lower Clime)
Dismounted, on th' *Aleian* Field I fall
Erroneous there to wander and forlorne.
Half yet remaines unsung, but narrower bound
Within the visible Diurnal Spheare;
Standing on Earth, not rapt above the Pole,
More safe I Sing with mortal voice, unchang'd
To hoarce or mute, though fall'n on evil dayes,

> On evil dayes though fall'n, and evil tongues;
> In darkness, and with dangers compast round,
> And solitude; yet not alone, while thou
> Visit'st my slumbers Nightly, or when Morn
> Purples the East: still govern thou my Song,
> *Urania*, and fit audience find, though few. (VII. 12-31)

This book, attentive as it is to the presence of *Urania* in each of the greatest of our poets, is designed to make you of that 'fit audience'. Johnson described the four invocations of *Paradise Lost* as 'beautiful' 'superfluities' (2000: 706). I agree that they are beautiful but do not think that they are superfluous. Hughes has argued that, 'By identifying himself... as Jaques' in *As You Like It*, 'Shakespeare converts his own name into a transitive phase' (1993: 102), and I think that the four invocations of *Paradise Lost* perform the same function for Milton. The process of writing the poem is also one of soul-making for the poet: the poem is divinely inspired (*Urania* 'visit'st my slumbers Nightly') but the labour of delivering the spirit of this poem is also Milton's way of presenting 'My true account': not an autobiography (as Wordsworth erroneously did in the *Prelude*) but a well-made soul that is to be broken by God from within. Milton, therefore, must be present within his poem: the poem is his ladder to God and his climbing of it is intended as an example for the braver readers or his spiritually 'fit audience, though few', to follow. 'My true account' is the kind of human creation out of which divine Creation breaks today: it is faithful activity, like writing a poem to 'assert Eternal Providence, | And justifie the wayes of God to men' (*Paradise Lost*, I. 25-6), or helping others in the world, that brings you to the wisdom of God, sister of *Urania*.

Milton was asserting Eternal Providence in the hopelessly old-fashioned genre of epic poetry, blind and in hiding, while the vogue at the Frenchified court of the newly restored King Charles was for plays and short satirical poems about fashion, drinking and sex; when, for example, the highly debauched John Wilmot, Earl of Rochester, would often go for a 'Ramble' in St James's Park to find prostitutes, taking care 'to see | Drunkenness Reliev'd by Leachery'; after 'Much wine had past with grave discourse, | Of who F-cks who and who does worse, | Such as you usually doe hear, | From those that diet at the *Beare*' (2010: 81).

In fact, Rochester's best poems record the defiant agonies of a fine soul confronting the very heart of nature, and I do not mean crudely to pitch 'the debauched Rochester' against 'the pure Milton', because the true poet's task is to transcend these seeming contraries, as Milton's very own 'evil dayes' are put to good use and transmuted by the soul-making activity of taking down his poem. Nonetheless, when Milton ends his invocation to Book VII of *Paradise Lost*, by imploring *Urania* to drive far off drunken revellers, he is channelling 'deep fears' (Milton 1998: 391):

> But drive farr off the barbarous dissonance
> Of *Bacchus* and his revellers, the Race
> Of that wilde Rout that tore the *Thracian* Bard
> In *Rhodope*, where Woods and Rocks had Eares
> To rapture, till the savage clamor dround
> Both Harp and Voice; nor could the Muse defend
> Her Son. So fail not thou, who thee implores:
> For thou art Heav'nlie, shee an empty dreame. (VII. 32-9)

Yeats's 'Crazy Jane' pointed out to the 'Bishop' that 'Love has pitched his mansion in | The place of excrement; | For nothing can be sole or whole | That has not been rent' (1950: 295). At the end of the decaying kind, Milton knows that his life has already been rent, but he prays for protection from violent death as he undertakes his project to make his soul whole, at the beginning of the unborn kind.

Orpheus is 'the *Thracian* Bard', type of all true or inspired poets. Eliade was 'certain that... shamanic elements persisted in the Thracian religion' and the myth of Orpheus 'displays several elements that can be compared to the shamanic ideology and techniques':

> his descent to Hades to bring back the soul of his wife, Eurydice... his healing art, his love for music and animals, his 'charms,' his power of divination. Even his character of 'culture hero' is not in contradiction to the best shamanic tradition – was not the 'first shaman' the messenger sent by God to defend humanity against diseases and to civilize it? (2004: 390 and 391)

One should think of Hermetic Occult Neoplatonism as a refined Renaissance version of shamanism. The practitioner, as microcosm of his society, embarks on spiritual journeys, down the primordial snake to the centre of this earth or up the spiritual ladder to God, to find out the cause of various maladies in the macrocosm of his culture. Shamans and Hermetic Occult Neoplatonists alike are '"those who walk the clouds"' (Eliade 2004: 390) as are the greatest of our poets. The shamanic or Neoplatonic elements in our poetry are vital to our culture especially when these roads to wisdom are mostly forgotten or no longer officially sanctioned.

Milton in *Paradise Lost* is also making the bold claim of this book: the practice of poetry is vital to the health of any culture; just as older societies relied on the shaman to diagnose and cure their ills. I am not maintaining that Milton was thinking of shamanism when he evoked 'the *Thracian* Bard'; he is refining his verse beyond such primitive practices so that it may adequately address the root of problems we face today in our own supposedly sophisticated, but decadent and decayed, Christian culture. By identifying himself with the isolated and despised Orpheus at the end of his life, Milton was also being realistic about his – and our – culture's devastating disregard of the significance of poetry for its own health. Earlier evocations of more triumphant aspects of Orpheus, by poets in the late sixteenth century, had demonstrated the same belief in the divine force of poetry, but also a greater optimism about its efficacy in our everyday world.

When the spirit of poetry manifests itself in a man to make him a poet, he is called to cleanse his soul in order to undertake such spiritual journeying as a shaman or alchemist – up and down Jaques' ladder – to diagnose and to try and cure our evils in the world today. My piety before the poetry I would explicate makes me say also that if you do not believe that the poet should fulfil such a vital, central and elevated role, then you are part of the problem: you have become too busy with business, or indeed revelling, in town to understand the voice of wisdom crying at its gates. You have become stone-like or beastly, and your very scepticism is one of the illnesses that the true poet must try and cure today.

Perennial wisdom from Spenser to Coleridge

Having made such bold claims about our future's dependence on poetry and talked for a chapter and a half about the greatest of our early modern poets, Shakespeare and Milton, this chapter, like Wordsworth's river in the *1805 Prelude*, 'Turns and will measure back his course' (IX. 5). Let us meander back to the late sixteenth century, when modern English poetry really came of age, in order to journey through the seventeenth and eighteenth centuries forward to the work of Blake and Coleridge, contemporaries of Wordsworth who stands at the beginning of this book, in the middle of things. During the sixteenth and seventeenth centuries there were a few great poets consciously attempting to fulfil the ancient curative function of poet. We will find that river of perennial wisdom, which courses through the generations, 'Run underground' (Yeats 1950: 275) for a spell, to rise again at the end of the eighteenth century in work that should still define our age today.

Edmund Spenser was married to Elizabeth Boyle on Midsummer's Day, 1594. His poem, *Epithalamion*, published that year, is essentially a wedding song, describing, in 24 Pindaric and Petrarchan stanzas, the pageantry and progression of his wedding day from his future wife's bedroom in the morning through the ceremony itself to their bridal chamber at night. It is hoped that the outcome is progeny; in another sense, all later English poets are Spenser's descendants.

Spenser solemnizes in poetry an occasion in his personal history for the good of all our futures; the very form of the poem takes on symbolic significance: its 24 stanzas and 365 interspersed long lines clearly denote the 24 hours of the wedding day and 365 days of the year of which it is part. 'However, we follow the linear progression of the events not by clock time, but by the phenomena of celestial light'. In turn, 'the poet treats the motion of sun, moon, and stars not merely as concurrent phenomena by which we measure human experience, but temporarily as active participants in the events of his wedding day, along with the various other participants from the whole range of natural and social orders' (1989: 661). Characteristically, Spenser acknowledges the temporary nature of this integration in our mutable world, imploring 'Phoebus, father of the Muse', 'But let this day let this one day be myne, | Let all the rest be thine' (*Epithalamion*, 121 and 125-6).

In the first stanza of the poem, Spenser addresses the Muses and evokes, as Milton will in his invocation to his 'Heav'nlie' Muse, that type of all poets, Orpheus:

Ye learned sisters which have oftentimes
Beene to me ayding, others to adorne:
Whom ye thought worthy of your gracefull rymes,
That even the greatest did not greatly scorne

> To heare theyr names sung in your simple layes,
> But joyed in theyr prayse.
> And when ye list your owne mishaps to mourne,
> Which death, or love, or fortunes wreck did rayse,
> Your string could soone to sadder tenor turne,
> And teach the woods and waters to lament
> Your dolefull dreriment.
> Now lay those sorrowfull complaints aside,
> And having all your heads with girland crownd,
> Helpe me mine own loves prayses to resound,
> Ne let the same of any be envide:
> So Orpheus did for his own bride,
> So I unto my selfe alone will sing,
> The woods shall to me answer and my Eccho ring. (1-18)

Orpheus' music had a supernatural power. During the Renaissance he was revered as a visionary seer as well as the archetypal lover-poet, his story found in Ovid, Virgil and Boethius. In fact, Spenser is making a specific allusion, in the final three lines of this first stanza of *Epithalamion*, to the moment in Virgil's account of the story when Orpheus mourns his wife's death from a snake-bite: 'he, solacing an aching heart with music from his hollow shell, sang of you to himself on the lonely shore, of you as day drew nigh, of you as day departed' (*Georgics*, IV. 646-6). After his prolonged singing, the poet-seer resolves to venture into Hades to win back his lost bride. In Spenser's poem the poet will also sing of his wife as day draws near and of her as day departed, but it seems odd initially that he should allude to the moment in Orpheus' story when he laments his wife's death.

It is well known that Spenser, influenced by Renaissance Neoplatonist interpretations of the mythic hero-lover as poet-prophet, 'presented himself as the English Orpheus, a vatic poet of love whose visions would move his countrymen to virtuous action' (Hamilton 1997: 519). I contend that the allusion to Orpheus' mournful singing connects the progress of *Epithalamion* with the journey of the mythic singer-seer to Hades, a connection which is reinforced by certain local details in Spenser's poem: for example, the 'rushy lake, | Where none doo fishes take' (60-1) is at once 'the small lake beside Kilcolman tower... Spenser's residence in Ireland', which 'is still "inhospitable to fish"' (Spenser 1989: 664), and 'the black ooze and unsightly reeds of Cocytus, the unlovely mere' (*Georgics*, IV. 478-9), which Orpheus passes on his way to the centre of the earth. Also, Spenser's inclusion of 'the people standing all about' (143), the crowds gathered to watch the wedding procession, in stanza 8, recalls Virgil's description of the crowds of 'insubstantial shades' who come from the lowest realms of Erebus, stirred by Orpheus' music (see *Georgics*, IV. 471-80). The central stanzas of Spenser's poem, which recount the marriage ceremony itself, are strangely presided over by the enchanted 'ruler of the shades' who says: '"We grant the man his wife to go with him, | Bought by his song"' (Boethius 2003: 309).

After Orpheus loses Eurydice a second time, by forgetting the King of the Ghost's caveat not to look back to his wife as they emerge from Hell, he mourns even more intensely her loss. Spenser's allusion is also to this second bout of sorrowful singing as it is related in Ovid:

> There was a hyll, and on the hyll a verie levell plot
> Fayre greene with grasse. But as for shade or covert was there not.
> Assoone as that this Poet borne of Goddes, in that same place
> Sate downe and toucht his tuned strings, a shadow came a pace.
> There wanted neyther *Chaons* tree, nor yit the trees too which
> Fresh *Phaetons* susters turned were, nor Beeche, nor Holme, nor Wiche,

* * *

> Such wood as this had *Orphye* drawen about him as among
> The herdes of beasts, and flocks of Birds he sate amyds the throng. (*Metamorphoses*, X. 93-97 and 148-9)

In Ovid's version, Orpheus' song magically creates the woods that shall to him answer, sheltering the entranced animals and birds. Spenser is implying that his verse has such creative power; his allusions to Boethius, Ovid and Virgil also give his poem twofold meaning. *Epithalamion* is at once a solemnization of the actual poet's historical wedding day and a description of an archetypal poet's mythical journey to the underworld.

Certainly the Orpheus that Spenser inherited was 'already heavy with interpretation. Early church fathers saw in him a pagan parallel to David the psalmist and pressed both into service as types of Christ' (Cain 1971: 24). I would argue that Spenser's use of myth is just as sophisticated as Joseph Campbell's understanding of the 'monomyth': the 'standard path of the mythological adventure of the hero'; 'a magnification of the formula represented in the rites of passage: *separation-initiation-return*' (1993: 30).

The centre of Spenser's poem, literally, with his bride at the altar in Church, is, spiritually speaking, his arrival '*at the nadir of the mythological round*'. The allusions to different versions of the Orpheus story plug *Epithalamion* into this archetypal journey: the hero-poet-seer '*undergoes a supreme ordeal and gains his reward*' and his '*triumph may be represented as the hero's sexual union with the goddess-mother of the world (sacred marriage)*'; '*intrinsically it is an expansion of consciousness and therewith of being (illumination, transfiguration, freedom). The final work is that of return*' to our everyday world (Campbell 1993: 246).

Spenser's poem weds him at once to Elizabeth Boyle and the Muse or 'Goddess of Complete Being' who 'unites the "good" and the "bad"' (Campbell 1993: 114): the poem is made to celebrate a real wedding in time and a poet-prophet's union with 'Cosmic Power, the totality of the universe, the harmonization of all the pairs of opposites, combining wonderfully the terror of absolute destruction with an impersonal yet motherly reassurance' (Campbell 1993: 115). Each poet that I would trace in this chapter, as a reincarnation of the spirit of poetry, is also such a journeying hero: 'the one who comes to know'. In Campbell's words:

> As he progresses from the slow initiation which is life, the form of the goddess undergoes for him a series of transfigurations: she can never be greater than himself, though she can always promise more than he is yet capable of comprehending. She lures, she guides, she bids him burst his fetters. (1993: 116)

Such is the sacred marriage solemnized by *Epithalamion*: it is an initiation, providing intimation that the poet is greater than he knows. The poetry itself is a kind of apotheosis of the poet as his self is drawn, like his poem, out of its everyday sphere into a realm of spiritual significance. In that first stanza of his marriage song, Spenser draws attention to his great allegorical poem, *The Faerie Queene,* of which three books had already been completed by 1594, and we should understand that *Epithalamion* also deploys allegory, connecting life in Queen Elizabeth's age with spiritual realms. As Spenser advises the Queen of England herself in *The Faerie Queene*:

> Of Faerie lond yet if he more inquire,
> By certaine signes here set in sundry place
> He may it find; ne let him then admire,
> But yield his sence to be too blunt and bace,
> That no'te without an hound fine footing trace.

And thou, O fairest Princesse under sky,
In this faire mirrhour maist behold thy face,
And thine owne realmes in lond of Faery,
And in this antique Image thy great auncestry. (II. Proem. 4)

In *The Defence of Poesie*, a prose tract first published in 1595, Sir Philip Sidney argues that learned men who inveigh against poetry are being ungrateful 'to seeke to deface that which in the noblest nations and language that are knowne, hath bene the first light giver to ignorance': do not such men 'play the Hedge-hogge, that being received into the den, drave out his host? Or rather the Vipers, that with their birth kill their parents?' In defending the art of poetry Sidney enlists the example of Orpheus since he was among the first of his 'country that made pennes deliverers of their knowledge to the posteritie', coming before them, 'as causes to draw with their charming sweetnesse the wild untamed wits to an admiration of knowledge': Orpheus was said 'to be listned to by beasts, indeed stonie and beastly people' (1968: sigs B2^{v}-B2^{r}). But posterity itself, forgetting poetry, can fall back into a stony and beastly state. As early modern reincarnations of the vagabond spirit of poetry, Spenser and Sidney hope to depetrify and humanize their contemporaries with their Orphic verse: 'for that same exquisite observing of number and measure in the words, and that high flying libertie of conceit propper to the Poet, did seeme to have some divine force in it' (Sidney 1968: sig. B4^{v}).

Sidney saw that 'the holy *Davids* Psalms are a divine poem' (1968: B4^{v}-B4^{r}), and in his translation of Psalm 42 asks,

Why art Thou my soul so sorry
And in me so much dismaid?
Wait on God, for yet his glory
In my song shall be display'd. (1962: 334)

Like Shakespeare, Sidney finds a fundamental connection between soul-making and poetry-making, although he finds that many of his contemporaries, blindly imitating the classics and Petrarch or merely searching out synonyms in dictionaries for their alliterative verse, 'do bewray a want of inward tuch' (1962: 172).

'Stella' is Sidney's name for Penelope Rich, in his sonnet sequence, *Astrophil and Stella,* which tells the story of his love for her during the years 1581-3; its origin in Latin also makes the name signify the Muse, that 'Cosmic Power' also at the centre of Spenser's *Epithalamion*: 'If *Orpheus*' voyce had force to breathe such musicke's love | Through pores of sencelesse trees, as it could make them move: |...| O stones, ô trees, learne hearing, *Stella* singeth' (1962: 208). It is implied that if we are beastly people, denying the divine force in poetry, then we are the stones and trees that Sidney addresses, objects charmed by Orpheus, but which were also eventually used by the bacchantes to destroy him. Thus the '*Third song*' of *Astrophil and Stella* expresses high hopes for poetry:

> The birds, beasts, stones and trees feel this, and feeling *Love*:
> And if the trees, nor stones stirre not the same to prove,
> Nor beasts, nor birds do come unto this blessed gaze,
> Know, that small Love is quicke, and great Love doth amaze:
> They are amaz'd, but you with reason armed,
> O eyes, ô eares of men, how are you charmed! (1962: 209)

The stones and trees do not move, not because they are not moved, but because they are too moved: without man's reason, they are amazed or stunned by the beauty of Stella's singing. All too often our senses are 'too blunt and bace', or too readily 'armed' with reason, which should not fight, but be charmed by, verse and song, to find 'Faerie lond', in this world, 'By certaine signes here set in sundry place'. Both Spenser and Sidney create poetry that can function as a mirror to show readers their ideal self from the future: 'There are mirrors and mirrors; and a work of imagination is a magic glass in which we may discover that nature to which actuality is barely an approximation' (Raine 1985: 160). Their poetry is intended to raise beastly people from their stony state, as Paulina's 'art' at the end of Shakespeare's *The Winter's Tale* transforms a statue of a maligned queen, who may in fact be already human, back into a human (see V. iii): the poet's art can make each of us a more humane human, to play on seventeenth-century spellings of that word.

In 'A nocturnall upon S. *Lucies* day, Being the shortest day', John Donne addresses the dark aspect of the 'Goddess of Complete Being', that 'Cosmic Power', ironically, as Lucy. In so doing, the poet becomes, paradoxically, more, by becoming less, human. Some critics have conjectured that the poem was prompted by Donne's wife's death in 1617, but the name, Lucie, would have conjured in the poet's mind his patroness, Lucy, Countess of Bedford: 'for Donne, the identity of one woman flowed into the other' (Donne 1990: xxix). The speaker of the poem, whoever that may be, is holding a vigil or night prayer on the eve of what used to be the shortest day of the year, according to the old calendar, at the onset of the winter solstice when the sun enters the sign of the Goat or Capricorn. This day, which is essentially like night, making Donne's title wittily appropriate, is also the festival of Santa Lucia, a third-century virgin martyr from Syracuse, 'who is ever associated by way of her name with light' (Donne 1991: 90) and blindness. In the northern hemisphere, the stars at the very beginning of her day are but 'light squibs':

> Tis the yeares midnight, and it is the dayes,
> *Lucies*, who scarce seaven houres herself unmaskes,
> The sunne is spent, and now his flasks
> Send forth light squibs, no constant rayes;

The worlds whole sap is sunke:
The generall balme th'hydroptique earth hath drunk,
Whither, as to the beds-feet life is shrunke,
Dead and enterr'd, yet all these seeme to laugh,
Compar'd with mee, who am their Epitaph.

Study me then, you who shall lovers bee
At the next world, that is, at the next Spring:
For I am every dead thing,
In whom love wrought new Alchimie.
For his art did expresse
A quintessence even from nothingnesse,
From dull privations, and leane emptinesse
He ruin'd mee, and I am re-begot
Of absence, darknesse, death; things which are not. (1991: 90-1)

'A quintessence' is the elusive fifth element, an elixir beyond earth, water, air and fire, which alchemists believed could cure all evils. In this case, love has inverted alchemical aspirations, arriving at an elixir of death or nothing, by working to essentialize forms of negativity. Through its evocation of such processes, 'A nocturnall' intensifies the poet's experience of 'the botome of Goddes secretes' (2009: 1 Corinthians 2. 10) on mother earth at the opposite end of the year to Shakespeare's *A Midsummer-Night's Dream*. Donne's epitaphic poem begins where Jaques' description of the seven ages of man leaves off; it comes after even 'second childishness, and meere oblivion, | Sans teeth, sans eyes, sans taste, sans every thing' (*As You Like It*, II. vii. 165-6). From the perspective of 'The young | In one another's arms' in this world ' – Those dying generations – ' (Yeats 1950: 217) such a starting place seems very bleak indeed. But another kind of lover might discover the poem's massive potential for spiritual re-begetting there. At the grave of the poet's everyday self, do we recognize from the future the benefit of nothing?

'I am by her death, (which word wrongs her) | Of the first nothing, the Elixer grown'; 'If I an ordinary nothing were, | As shadow' (not even one of the player-shadows of *A Midsummer-Night's Dream*, but just a shady patch) 'a light, and body must be here':

> But I am None; nor will my Sunne renew.
> You lovers, for whose sake, the lesser Sunne
>   At this time to the Goat is runne
>   To fetch new lust, and give it you,
>   Enjoy your summer all,
> Since shee enjoyes her long nights festivall,
> Let mee prepare towards her, and let me call
> This houre her Vigill, and her eve, since this
> Both the yeares, and the dayes deep midnight is. (1991: 91-2)

I can still remember John Carey admitting in a seminar, perhaps wisely, that he couldn't get to the bottom of this poem. I have come to see that it articulates Campbell's insight:

> Woman is the guide to the sublime acmes of sensuous adventure. By deficient eyes she is reduced to inferior states; by the evil eye of ignorance she is spellbound to banality and ugliness. But she is redeemed by the eyes of understanding. The hero who can take her as she is, without undue commotion but with the kindness and assurance she requires, is potentially the king, the incarnate god, of her created world. (1993: 116)

'A nocturnall' unfolds perhaps out of a domestic tragedy, but it also unfolds itself potentially as a cosmic comedy; it calls for such explication ('Study me then'): the nothingness at the core of man's being expresses itself at the end of the decaying kind that must precede the beginning of the unborn kind. We can think of the relationship between Donne and Lucy as expressing at once relations between man and wife, immortal soul and earthy matter or nature, and god and world. Most importantly, the poem essentializes, one might say, quintessentializes, the preparing, which we also discerned in Spenser's *Epithalamion*, of poet, as reincarnation of the spirit of poetry, towards the cosmic Muse: in these poems, the hero is learning to take her as she is, for good and for bad, in sickness and in health, so that he can become god of her created world, thus redeeming her by the eyes of understanding. By writing 'A nocturnall', Donne gets to the dark heart of this matter:

Oft a flood
Have wee two wept, and so
Drownd the whole world, us two; oft did we grow
To be two Chaosses, when we did show
Care to ought else; and often absences
Withdrew our soules, and made us carcasses. (1991: 91)

The lovers' previous sadnesses, their neglect of each other, and 'separations, which parted their bodies but not their souls, so that their bodies remained mere shells', have repeated backwards in microcosm Biblical time; 'they themselves were the world which their mutual grief drowned' (Donne 1996: 392) and from such a flood, they have proceeded to the deep at the beginning of the Bible. By her 'death, (which word wrongs her)', the poem is 'Of the first nothing', the nothing out of which God created the world, and which is at the heart of our being.

George Herbert's 'Affliction IV', first published in 1633, contains a metaphor within a metaphor, which at once describes such an afflicted state and makes it a part of spiritual growth:

Broken in pieces all asunder,
Lord, hunt me not,

A thing forgot
Once a poor creature, now a wonder,
A wonder tortur'd in the space
Betwixt this world and that of grace.

My thoughts are all a case of knives,
Wounding my heart
With scatter'd smart,
As watring pots give flowers their lives.
Nothing their furies can controll,
While they do wound and pink my soul. (1978: 89-90)

Like the mysterious speaker of Donne's poem, Herbert speaks as 'a wonder' who was once, but is no longer, 'a creature': he speaks out of the first nothing, which has its use today, when it is acknowledged as vital to any man's life: 'Nothing their furies can controll' means, literally speaking, that there is not anything that can control the furies of his thoughts, but also, spiritually speaking, that nothing itself has the capability of controlling those soul-wounding thoughts. The poet's meditation in verse on nothing, undermining the discourse of language, can help to quieten his mind so that his everyday self becomes capable of living with God that dwells within.

Our thoughts become especially painful when we are on the verge of giving them up, at the end of the decaying kind; and our very consciousness of the painfulness of consciousness helps to nurture in our hearts the peace of unconscious faith, at the beginning of the unborn kind. Then the case of knives functions like the diffused water from a watering can, giving us life. As Stanley Fish has said of Herbert's poems, 'they perform what they require of us, for as they undermine our reliance on discursive forms of thought, and urge us to rest in the immediate apprehension of God's all-effective omnipresence, they become the vehicles of their own abandonment': Herbert 'baptizes language by making it subversive of its usual functions' (1972: 158 and 159).

Surrounded by our things in this world, it is a prospect full of afflictions to accept the benefit of nothing. Both Donne and Herbert are recording in verse the painful process of purging themselves of 'spots of time' (Wordsworth, *1799 Prelude,* I. 288), subverting rational discourse, in order to find that eternal 'moment in each day' (Blake, *Milton,* Plate 35. 42-5); the speakers of their poems come to nothing, which makes each, not just a broken creature, but a wonder, creating anew in verse the universe from the future, 'the abode where the Eternal are' (Shelley 2003: 545): 'Nothing performs the task of life: | The elements are let loose to fight, | And while I live, trie out their right'. Caught up in such Chaos, the poet exclaims 'O help, my God':

Then shall those powers, which work for grief,
Enter thy pay,
And day by day
Labour thy praise, and my relief;
With care and courage building me,
Till I reach heav'n, and much more, thee. (1978: 90)

In 'The Water-fall', first published in 1655, Henry Vaughan contemplates the necessary evil of the immortal soul's falling to earth, this sea of time and space, in lines that deepen the spiritual insights of English poets of the 1590s:

With what deep murmurs through times silent stealth
Doth thy transparent, cool and watry wealth
Here flowing fall,
And chide, and call,
As if his liquid, loose Retinue staid
Lingring, and were of this steep place afraid,

> The common pass
> Where, clear as glass,
> All must descend
> Not to an end:
> But quickned by this deep and rocky grave,
> Rise to a longer course more bright and brave.

Donne imagines lovers weeping and so flooding the whole world, Herbert thinks of his thoughts as a case of knives becoming the baptismal fall of water through the head of a watering can, and Vaughan contemplates a waterfall to meditate on the necessity of suffering in this world so that each spark of divine intelligence has the opportunity to make a fully individuated soul in God, out of the first nothing:

> What sublime truths, and wholesome themes,
> Lodge in thy mystical, deep streams!
> Such as dull man can never finde
> Unless that Spirit lead his minde
> Which first upon thy face did move,
> And hatch'd all with his quickning love. (1957: 537 and 538)

All of the poets in this chapter so far acknowledge that an ordinary life must be rent, so that it may be made whole in God. Such a process transforms a melancholy creature into an inspired wonder, that Spirit that moved upon the deep, moving upon the deep of man's soul each day, to express in poetry and in a life 'The greater Heaven in an Heaven less' (Marvell 1971: 1. 12). Each of these poets functions potentially as a shaman might in an older culture: each, as a reincarnation of the spirit of poetry, is a hero-lover and poet-prophet, capable of journeying to the centre of the earth or to the heavens, to bring back knowledge from the silence at the heart of our being in order to cure our modern ills. The art of poetry foregrounds and transforms the everyday discursive life of language, each of us reborn potentially in a medium that allows you, 'Before death come' to 'Walk to the skie | Even in this life' (Vaughan 1957: 483); our divine imagination putting human reason to soul-making work through the turning of verse in this world.

The stream of perennial wisdom that we have been tracing as it falls through these poets runs underground during the eighteenth century. Certainly one can find reincarnations of Milton's 'Il Penseroso' in the figures constrained by Thomas Gray's 'Elegy Written in a Country Church Yard' and Oliver Goldsmith's 'The Deserted Village'. But they are enfolded by a 'darkness' and 'desolation' (Gray, Collins and Goldsmith 1976: 117 and 677) that almost overwhelms. Certainly Alexander Pope's '*Sylphs*', the 'unnumber'd Spirits' of 'The light *Militia* of the lower sky', in *The Rape of the Lock* (I. 41 and 42) and 'ye gentle powers | Of musical delight' that 'dance around' the 'strain' of Mark Akenside's *The Pleasures of Imagination* (I. 6-7 and 8) are the same in kind as the 'Millions of spiritual Creatures' that 'walk the Earth | Unseen', 'Singing thir great Creator: oft in bands | While they keep watch', in Milton's *Paradise Lost* (IV. 677-8 and 684-5) and 'Ye Elves of hils, brooks, standing lakes & groves' over which Prospero finally renounces control in Shakespeare's *The Tempest* (V. i. 33). But Pope and Akenside come close to treating these forces, still potent in Shakespeare and Milton, as merely fanciful or literary ornaments, of interest only for their classical associations. Nonetheless it is out of this 'sub-classical' (Jonathan Wordsworth 1984: 40) tradition of English poetry that Blake, Coleridge and Wordsworth make their fresh poems of supernatural potency, capable of healing a sick society.

In *The Golden Treasury*, Francis Palgrave traced the same river that we have been following in our meandering chronology of English poetry so far. The fourth and final book of his famous anthology picks up that story in the late eighteenth century; its first poem is Blake's 'To the Muses'. In that poem, first published in 1783, Blake expresses his dismay at the state of poetry in his own time and asks of the Muses:

> How have you left the ancient love
> That bards of old enjoy'd in you!
> The languid strings do scarcely move,
> The sound is forced, the notes are few. (Palgrave 1913: 197)

Palgrave is using the poem no doubt to comment on the quality of some of the poems of the eighteenth century from his perspective in the late nineteenth century: Blake's poem heralds a new golden age for poetry in Britain. We shall see in the next chapter how Blake transforms the poetry of his day, providing potentially for future generations of poets. The undercurrent of perennial wisdom that flows through the generations certainly surfaced in Blake, Wordsworth, Coleridge, Shelley and Keats during the late eighteenth and early nineteenth centuries. But we shall see it run underground again towards the end of the nineteenth century.

One night in February 1798 Coleridge transformed the semi- or quasi-melancholy state of the speaker in Book IV of William Cowper's 1785 poem, *The Task*. Cowper had celebrated sitting alone, day-dreaming by a fire, 'in parlour twilight: such a gloom | Suits well the thoughtful and unthinking mind, | The mind contemplative, with some new theme | Pregnant, or indispos'd alike to all' (IV. 278-81). Coleridge's 'Frost at Midnight' acts as poetic midwife to this part of *The Task*, delivering from Cowper's lines that with which they are pregnant: apprehension of the divine imagination at work or at play in man. Cowper describes how he can:

> lose an hour
> At ev'ning, till at length the freezing blast,
> That sweeps the bolted shutter, summons home

The recollected pow'rs; and, snapping short
The glassy threads, with which the fancy weaves
Her brittle toys, restores me to myself. (IV. 302-7).

Coleridge, left alone with his slumbering 'cradled infant', by a dying fire in his cottage parlour at midnight, does not find the darkness and desolation of Gray's and Goldsmith's elegies, but explores instead his 'Abstruser musings' to become a new kind of *Il Penseroso,* prophesying the spiritual potential of our late modern age. His 'idling Spirit | By its own moods interprets, every where | Echo or mirror seeking of itself, | And makes a toy of Thought' (2001: 1. 454). The poet is not snapped out of such meditation by the weather outside, like Cowper, but is restored to a potentially greater self, by recalling moments from his own childhood, in order to think ahead to his child's future education in the countryside, probably in the Lake District. We have seen how Milton's scholar in 'Il Penseroso' aims to learn directly from the spirit of Hermes Trismegistus, now Coleridge envisages his growing child being taught by God directly through nature:

so shalt thou see and hear
The lovely shapes and sounds intelligible
Of that eternal language, which thy God
Utters, who from eternity doth teach
Himself in all, and all things in himself.
Great universal Teacher! he shall mould
Thy spirit, and by giving make it ask. (2001: 1. 456)

A few months' later, in July 1798, Wordsworth will write the lines with which this book began, reposing under a 'dark sycamore' in the Wye Valley. Neither poet is darkly love sick, instead in their newly invented form, the 'Conversation Poem', each finds himself able to articulate their shared feelings of 'A presence that disturbs me with the joy | Of elevated thoughts; a sense sublime

| Of something far more deeply interfused' (Wordsworth 2009: 1. 374-5), rediscovering the divine power of imagination in man that can respond to, as it is interfused with, the 'Goddess of Complete Being' in nature. With Blake, Wordsworth and Coleridge in the 1790s this book has reached again that high point of English poetry, the spirit of which we now call 'Romantic', matching in its soul-making exuberance the hopes of certain English poets in the 1590s. What darkness lies ahead for future incarnations of the spirit of poetry?

Chapter 5

What Hope Does a Modern Poet Have?

W. B. Yeats

In September 1938, not long before his death and the Second World War, Yeats articulated his creed, revising rough lines into one of his last great poems, 'Under Ben Bulben'. After Yeats's death his wife decided that this unpublished climactic poem should stand at the very end of the 'Lyrical' section of his *Collected Poems*. Later editors have realized that it was intended to be the first of his *Last Poems* so that the others appear to be spoken posthumously. The poem is intended to make sure that the poet will be buried as he wishes, ending at it does with what will be his epitaph; it also essentializes the core of Yeats's convictions:

Many times man lives and dies
Between his two eternities,
That of race and that of soul,
And ancient Ireland knew it all.
Whether man die in his bed
Or the rifle knocks him dead,
A brief parting from those dear
Is the worst man has to fear.
Though grave-diggers' toil is long,
Sharp their spades, their muscles strong,
They but thrust their buried men
Back in the human mind again. (1950: 398)

At this point in his life, Yeats understood, with some trepidation as his struck through and interpolated words indicate, that: 'I am old & ill | my flesh is heavy it weighs upon my | heart but I shall soon cast it off | be ~~as light as~~ if god wills I shall | be as light as a tred of cotton' (Yeats 1997: 5). The poet believed in metempsychosis and had taken great pains while he was still alive to investigate different phases of the transmigration of the soul; he was intensely curious about the progress and temporary transformations of 'age-long memoried self' (Yeats 1980: 272) as it makes its journeys from one body to another. The vagabond spirit of poetry that we have been tracing in its various incarnations across the generations is an aspect of 'The bright eternal Self that is everywhere'; 'that is immortality, that is Spirit, that is all' (Yeats and Swami 1970: 135). Any poet lives between that eternity and that of his race in whose language soul must become manifest.

In section IV of 'Under Ben Bulben', Yeats offers a potted history of art, which is also a record of different incarnations of that immortal soul through the generations, from the ancient Egyptian period to the 1830s when 'Confusion fell upon our thought' (1950: 400). He begins by admonishing modern artists, including poets, to continue with the soul-making work of tradition:

> Poet and sculptor, do the work,
> Nor let the modish painter shirk
> What his great forefathers did,
> Bring the soul of man to God,
> Make him fill the cradles right. (1950: 399)

Art performs its function between man's 'two eternities | That of race and that of soul'. In Yeats's opinion our culture is decayed and decadent; in order to rejuvenate the arts today, it is necessary at first to look before. Yeats calls for a Renaissance of the future that comprehends not only Roman and Greek models, but the very beginnings of human civilization. Any artist today should first school himself in tradition, which teaches its adepts that it is to be understood as the record of divine revelation in time. Then the look before becomes a looking after of mankind into eternity, which will have come to us from the future:

> Measurement began our might:
> Forms a stark Egyptian thought,
> Forms that gentler Phidias wrought. (1950: 399)

Yeats's later poems are also based on measurement: on the rhythm or numbers of traditional verse and on symbolic foundations, worked out before their geometric lineaments are covered over with pleasing naturalistic details. Such a method of composition implies that the poet believed all natural forms to be the expression of God on earth, the realism of his verse expressing for the initiated the ideals of divine order. As Plotinus argued:

> Still the arts are not to be slighted on the ground that they create by imitation of natural objects; for, to begin with, these natural objects are themselves imitations; then, we must recognize that they give no bare reproductions of the thing seen but go back to the Reason-Principles from which Nature itself derives, and, furthermore, that much of their work is all their own; they are holders of beauty and add where nature is lacking. Thus Pheidias wrought the Zeus upon no model among things of sense but by apprehending what form Zeus must take if he chose to become manifest to sight. (1992: 486; V. 8. 1)

Like the greatest sculptors and painters of tradition, and quite unlike modern novelists, Yeats models in verse, not an imitation of 'the bundle of accident and incoherence that sits down to breakfast' (1961: 509), but 'the "Divine Human", "Jesus the Imagination"' (Raine 1991: 13), our greater future self, the form that God must take if He has indeed chosen to become manifest in man. Section IV of 'Under Ben Bulben' continues by jumping ahead to the premature climax of its history of art when man is 'reborn as an idea, something intended, complete' (Yeats 1961: 509) on a ceiling in Rome:

> Michael Angelo left a proof
> On the Sistine Chapel roof,
> Where but half-awakened Adam
> Can disturb globe-trotting Madam
> Till her bowels are in heat,
> Proof that there's a purpose set
> Before the secret working mind:
> Profane perfection of mankind. (1950: 399)

The purpose set before each incarnation of the spirit of poetry is to perfect mankind in time. In this world of generation the secret working mind must labour to apprehend what form God must take here, married as He is in man's creative imagination to nature or the 'Goddess of Complete Being':

> Quattrocento put in paint
> On backgrounds for a God or Saint
> Gardens where a soul's at ease;
> Where everything that meets the eye,
> Flowers and grass and cloudless sky,
> Resemble forms that are or seem
> When sleepers wake and yet still dream,
> And when it's vanished still declare,
> With only bed and bedstead there,
> That heavens had opened. (1950: 399)

Hughes's central argument about Shakespeare's work can be applied directly to Yeats's poetry, which is always 'essentially dramatic' (Brown 1999: x):

> By constructing his basic Equation out of living myth, he is able to create dramas, which, no matter how secular they seem, or how real in the dimension of external historic event and of psychology, nevertheless embody and communicate a very particular 'mythic' dimension, which is to say a 'divine' or 'daemonic' dimension. (1993: 3)

Yeats's mythic equation, the measurement that begins his might, is constructed out of two interlocking 'gyres', 'the apex of each vortex in the middle of the other's base' (1962: 68). Such a symbol, which comprehends even the relation between history and myth that Hughes describes, was revealed to Yeats by his 'instructors', that is, by spirits who began to communicate to the poet through his wife's automatic writing on their honeymoon in 1917.

These interlocking cones represent vast cycles of history: in our modern age 'the gyre of "Concord" diminishes as that of "Discord" increases', but from within that age, one can imagine afterwards 'the gyre of "Concord" increasing while that of "Discord" diminishes, and so on, one gyre within the other always. Here the thought of Heraclitus dominates all: "Dying each other's life, living each other's death"' (1962: 68). At the base of the gyre of the decaying kind, the poet imagines the apex of the gyre of the unborn kind of time. These two interlocking spirals can also be made to represent the difference between love and strife, our illusions of subjectivity and objectivity, the play of declaration and irony in Yeats's work, and the conflict between faith and scepticism in our age. Such gyres, it turns out, run through the condensed history of art that Yeats has been tracing:

> Gyres run on;
> When that greater dream had gone
> Calvert and Wilson, Blake and Claude,
> Prepared a rest for the people of God,

> Palmer's phrase, but after that
> Confusion fell upon our thought. (1950: 400)

Richard Wilson and Claude Lorrain created idyllic Italianate landscapes in the eighteenth and seventeenth centuries respectively, which can be seen as continuations of the tradition that had climaxed earlier in the figures of Michelangelo, his own idealizations deeply influenced by the painters, Neoplatonist philosophers and poets of fifteenth-century Florence. Samuel Palmer was captivated by Blake's small but masterfully vivid illustrations for a school edition of Virgil, his 'visions of little dells, and nooks, and corners of Paradise':

> There is in all such a mystic dreamy glimmer as penetrates and kindles the inmost soul, and gives complete and unreserved delight, unlike the gaudy daylight of this world. They are like all that wonderful artist's works the drawing aside of the fleshly curtain, and the glimpse which all the most holy, studious saints and sages have enjoyed, of that rest which remaineth to the people of God. (Palmer 1972: 15-6)

'Palmer's phrase' is, in fact, to be found also in Hebrews: 'There remaineth... a rest to the people of God' (4. 9). The influence of Blake's later illustrations is palpable in Palmer's own work up until about 1834, as well as in Edward Calvert's, another young disciple of the old engraver-poet-prophet who died in 1827. But after the 1830s, in Yeats's opinion, western art became merely symptomatic of the gyre of discord increasing, and he foresaw that our own age today could only become increasingly confused as one kind of time is currently in the process of preceding another that has already begun. As Yeats makes 'Balzac, that great eater' say, in response to Hegel's exposition of the progress of history:

> There is a continual conflict – I too have my dialectic – the perfection of Nature is the decline of Spirit, the perfection of Spirit is the decline of Nature. In the Spiritual dawn when Raphael painted the Camera della Segnatura, and the Medician Popes dreamed of uniting Christianity and Paganism, all that was sacred with all that was secular, Europe might have made its plan, begun the solution of its problems, but individualism came instead; the egg instead of hatching, burst. (1961: 467-8)

The 'work' that Yeats would have the poet, sculptor and painter do 'fabricates all things into "an homogenous sphere"' in the midst of our modern discord, 'but even the sphere formed by Concord is not the changeless eternity, for Concord or Love but offers us the image of that which is changeless' (1962: 67-8). Yeats's 'fabricates' denotes the labour of construction, in metal, stone, wood or words (as Yeats well knew, it is easier to 'break stones | Like an old pauper, in all kinds of weather' (1950: 89) than to make lasting poetry), but the word also implies another kind of making up: the necessary fiction of art that would apprehend the beginning of the unborn kind of time already at the end of the decaying kind of time: 'We are part of a fraicheur, inaccessible | Or accessible only in the most furtive fiction' (Stevens 1990: 120).

Making up, 'With faining voice, verses of faining love', the ideal poet helps to make up our soul in the future, so that we may endure now an impending cycle of history; the work of Shakespeare and of Yeats performs the necessary and dramatic function of allowing us to see, in the late modern age, 'things with parted eye, | When every things seems double', like Hermia, prototype of a new kind of initiate, at the end of *A Midsummer-Night's Dream* (I. i. 31 and IV. i. 193-4). Such work might still hatch the egg of the Renaissance, the 'Spiritual dawn' of our age when Bottom awoke from his 'rare vision' (*A Midsummer-Night's Dream,*

IV. i. 209) and Prospero, at the top of Jaques' ladder, understood that he must abjure his 'rough magic' (*The Tempest*, V. i. 50).

When confusion fell upon our thought

In the early summer of 1821, ten or so years before our poetry, art and thought became confused and infected by the ever-increasing gyre of discord, Shelley at once lamented Keats's death and unwittingly predicted his own drowning off the shore of Lerici. The final verse of 'Adonais' echoes Milton's invocation of *Urania* in Book VII of *Paradise Lost*:

> The breath whose might I have invoked in song
> Descends on me; my spirit's bark is driven
> Far from the shore, far from the trembling throng
> Whose sails were never to the tempest given;
> The massy earth and sphered skies are riven!
> I am borne darkly, fearfully, afar;
> Whilst burning through the inmost veil of Heaven,
> The soul of Adonais, like a star,
> Beacons from the abode where the Eternal are. (2003: 545)

Shelley's soul is still afloat on the tempest-driven sea of time and space, but he is navigating his passage through life and our history according to Keats's bright Pole Star, emblem of 'something intended, complete', which directs him back to Heaven due north. Like Blake and Palmer, Shelley believed that:

> Poetry defeats the curse which binds us to be subjected to the accident of surrounding impressions. And whether it spreads its own figured curtain or withdraws life's dark veil from before the scene of things, it equally creates for us a being within our being. It makes us the inhabitants of a world to which the familiar world is as a chaos. It reproduces the common Universe of which we are portions and percipients,

> and it purges from our inward sight the film of familiarity which obscures from us the wonder of our being. It compels us to feel that which we perceive, and to imagine that which we know. (2003: 698)

After Shelley's death, poets seemed less sure of poetry's power to create 'anew the universe after it has been annihilated in our minds by the recurrence of impressions blunted by reiteration' (2003: 698). Lamenting the death of his close friend Arthur Hallam, just as confusion was falling on our thought in the 1830s, Alfred Lord Tennyson lingered one night on the lawn after his companions had gone to bed, and found himself 'whirl'd | About empyreal heights of thought' until he 'caught | The deep pulsations of the world, | Aeonian music measuring out | The steps of Time – the shocks of Chance – | The blows of Death'. However, 'At length my trance | Was cancell'd, stricken thro' with doubt' (*In Memoriam*, XCV), his apprehension of the One Life overwhelmed by the increasing gyre of chaos, or that which Yeats called 'this filthy modern tide' (1950: 376).

Robert Browning in the 1850s could involve his readers ingeniously in this drama of doubt and perplexities, asking us to help him hold:

> a thought, I know,
> Has tantalized me many times,
> (Like turns of thread the spiders throw
> Mocking across our path) for rhymes
> To catch at and let go.

But 'Then the good minute goes' (1940: 237 and 238), and we realize that the poet is concerned with fleeting or Wordsworthian 'spots of time', rather than a Blakeian 'moment in the day', which renovates all other moments of that day:

> Just when I seemed about to learn!
> Where is the thread now? Off again!
> The old trick! Only I discern –
> Infinite passion, and the pain
> Of finite hearts that yearn. (1940: 238)

As we have seen, in an early draft of 'Under Ben Bulben', Yeats reassures himself, near death, that he shall soon cast off his ailing body and 'be ~~as light as~~ if god wills I shall | be as light as a tred of cotton', the struck through words and interpolation of 'if god wills' poignantly indicating his niggling doubts about the nature of Purgatory. His verse too is a thread of cotton to wind as we tread our way out of our modern labyrinth, offered in the spirit that Blake gives his readers in his poetry 'the end of a golden string', which can lead us in at 'Heavens gate' (*Jerusalem*, Plate 77). Browning's verse, caught up like Yeats's with the yearning of a finite heart, but without Yeats's sense of the larger visionary picture, can only catch at such a thread within its labyrinth: not finding Ariadne's golden string but only 'turns of thread the spiders throw', Browning's verse all too often looks before rather than after; it is a fine soul's articulation of, and invitation to become involved with, the complexities of our dark and chaotic age.

Matthew Arnold evoked a semi-mythical version of *Il Penseroso* in 'The Scholar Gypsy', a poem about a poor Oxford scholar who abandoned his degree to live with gypsies. Lying in a boat, 'Moor'd to the cool bank in the summer-heats', in the early 1850s, the poet has watched 'the warm, green-muffled Cumner hills', and wondered if this ancient figure, emblematic of an age of concord, still 'haunt'st their shy retreats' (1929: 275):

> – No, no thou has not felt the lapse of hours!
> For what wears out the life of mortal men?
> 'Tis that from change to change their being rolls;

'Tis that repeated shocks, again, again,
Exhaust the energy of strongest souls
And numb the elastic powers.
Till having used our nerves with bliss and teen,
And tired upon a thousand schemes our wit,
To the just-pausing Genius we remit
Our worn-out life, and are – what we have been.

Thou hast not lived, why should'st thou perish, so?
Thou hadst *one* aim, *one* business, *one* desire;
Else wert thou long since number'd with the dead! (1929: 277-8)

In the mid nineteenth century man could not keep up with Blake's figures, which 'have that intense, soul-evidencing attitude and action, and that elastic, nervous spring which belongs to uncaged immortal spirits'. Towards the end of that century the artist's 'Excess' was not 'the essential vivifying spirit, vital spark, embalming spice... of the finest art' (Palmer 1972: 16), but an affected and slightly bored decadence. By 1891, Wilde could assert, 'All art is quite useless' (2003: 17). No wonder Arnold had implored his scholar-gypsy to 'Fly hence, our contact fear' (1929: 279)! At the beginning of the twentieth century the gyre of discord had so increased that Romanticism itself was badly infected, and T. E. Hulme, for example, could celebrate in 1911 the 'classical in verse':

> even in the most imaginative flights there is always holding back, a reservation. The classical poet never forgets this finiteness, this limit of man. He remembers always that he is mixed up with earth... I object even to the best of the romantics. I object still more to the receptive attitude. I object to the sloppiness which doesn't consider that a poem is a poem unless it is moaning or whining about something or other... I prophesy that a period of dry, hard, classical verse is coming. (Greenblatt 2006: 2. 2001-2)

Hulme was only half right in his prediction. Certainly poets like Pound and Eliot adopted a drier and harder style after the First World War. But the greatest poetry of the twentieth century remains, although it might not seem so at first, Romantic.

Wallace Stevens

Yeats composed much of his best work after such Modernist manifestoes as Hulme's, in the wake of Eliot's *The Waste Land*. With some help from Ezra Pound and his own esoteric investigations, the dandyish poet of the Rhymers' Club, *The Celtic Twilight* and the Abbey Theatre transformed himself to write a kind of poetry, in which the poet remembers that he is mixed up with earth, but that he also contains the infinite. It is perhaps more surprising that it took Wallace Stevens, the Vice President of the Hartford Accident and Indemnity Company, a man one would imagine 'tired upon a thousand schemes', to evoke in verse of fine vivifying excess, figures of capable imagination, which 'have that intense, soul-evidencing attitude and action'. In just this spirit he will have us hear the half-light-hearted 'poet's prayer' in 'Sailing after Lunch':

> The romantic should be here.
> The romantic should be there.
> It ought to be everywhere.
> But the romantic must never remain,
>
> Mon Dieu, and must never again return. (1954: 120)

We hear such a prayer answered, or at least rearticulated, at the very end of the poet's life in 'Final Soliloquy of the Interior Paramour', the beginning of a 'long poem' (Stevens 1996: 701) never finished, but chosen by Stevens to conclude his 1953 *Selected Poems*, and to precede the title poem of his last collection, 'The Rock', first published under his supervision at the end of his *Collected Poems* in 1954:

> Light the first light of evening, as in a room
> In which we rest and, for small reason, think
> The world imagined is the ultimate good. (1954: 524)

The poem prepares for and presents 'the intensest rendezvous' between 'the "Divine Human"' or '"Jesus the Imagination"' and the 'Goddess of Complete Being' or the Muse, which we have seen also expressed in terms of Apuleius' Ass and Isis, Bottom and Titania, Astrophil and Stella, Spenser and his bride, Donne and Lucy, and Wordsworth and nature. During such a rendezvous there is felt 'A light, a power, the miraculous influence':

> Here, now, we forget each other and ourselves.
> We feel the obscurity of an order, a whole,
> A knowledge, that which arranged the rendezvous.
>
> Within its vital boundary, in the mind.
> We say God and the imagination are one...
> How high that highest candle lights the dark. (1954: 524)

This poem is of that which 'is in Herself pure blissful Consciousness... is also the Mother of Nature and is Nature itself born of the creative play of Her thought': such 'faith... is... in some of its essential features one of the oldest and most wide-spread religions in the world' (Avalon 2008: 124). The poem is also of a man who believed that 'A force capable of bringing about fluctuations in reality in words free from mysticism is a force independent of one's desire to elevate it. It needs no elevation. It has only to be presented, as best one is able to present it' (1960: viii). The poem is at once the poet's final soliloquy about the interior paramour and the final soliloquy that she speaks: it is a soliloquy that hides a colloquy during which 'we forget each other and ourselves'.

Stevens' later poetry concerns itself with the evasions of language in relation to 'pure blissful Consciousness', or that which certain philosophers have labelled 'being'. The poet comes to an understanding of this force as that which loves to conceal itself: the interest of his poems is in 'a mode of being-manifest, i.e. of *unhiddenness,* which in itself is simultaneously, and indeed essentially, *hiddenness;* a truth to whose essence there belongs un-truth' (Heidegger 2004: 227). His work demonstrates that there is a force in language, which maintains, proffers and enriches relations between order and chaos, imagination and reality, man and nature, while holding itself in reserve; such work is also playful: it hides that which loves to hide, because its continued concealment makes it continuously unconcealable, not merely correct.

Stevens' later poetry also collects itself out of his own and others' earlier poems. Such correspondence between poems is not necessarily dependent on individual memory; 'that which arranged the rendezvous' between poets, 'that age-long memoried self', penetrating with its light all it has gathered, hatches poetic identities, by making their work greater than they knew. Then explication can rejoice 'in the light of clear perception at beholding with each new birth' of the spirit of poetry, 'the human race... work for itself new organs of power appropriate to the new sphere of its motion and activity' (Coleridge 1849: 1. 31-2). Stevens' poems conceal such joyful or 'pure explication de texte', which may be after all the poet's 'principal form of piety' (Stevens 1996: 793).

From the perspective of our world we discern poetic influence as if it flows from the past when in reality it discloses on earth the future in eternity. Ultimately, or anagogically speaking, poetic influence denotes the miraculous influence. Stevens' greatest poems are not 'Formd by the Daughters of Memory'; he writes 'Surrounded by the daughters of Inspiration' (Blake 2008:

554). The poet's care to let his poems present the force that withdraws, 'the obscurity of an order', makes his poetry distinctive; that evasive power also gives his poems affinities with the work of other poets so committed. In distinctive ways, great poets speak from the same source; their work gives 'Expression ever varying' to the same 'moving soul' (Wordsworth, *1850 Prelude*: vi. 15 and *1805 Prelude*, XIII. 171) that is 'within us and abroad' (Coleridge 2001: 1. 233).

In 'Final Soliloquy', 'We say God and the imagination are one', the speaker of the poem speaking, presumably, for himself, his paramour and his ideal reader. Who else says such a thing?

At the beginning of *Jerusalem*, Blake confesses:

> Trembling I sit day and night, my friends are astonish'd at me.
> Yet they forgive my wanderings, I rest not from my great task!
> To open the Eternal Worlds, to open the immortal Eyes
> Of Man inwards into the Worlds of Thought: into Eternity
> Ever expanding in the Bosom of God. the Human Imagination
> O Saviour pour upon me thy Spirit of meekness & love:
> Annihilate the Selfhood in me, be thou all my life! (Plate 5)

In 'A Vision of The Last Judgment', he gives his most developed definition of the 'Imagination', glossing these lines from *Jerusalem*, and saying expressly that this faculty is one with God:

> This world of Imagination is the World of Eternity it is the Divine bosom into which we shall all go after the death of the Vegetated body This World <of Imagination> is Infinite & Eternal whereas the world of Generation or Vegetation is Finite & [*for a small moment*] Temporal. There Exist in that Eternal World the Permanent Realities of Every Thing which we see reflected in this Vegetable Glass of Nature All Things are comprehended in their Eternal Forms in the Divine body of the Saviour the True Vine of Eternity The Human

> Imagination who appeard to Me as Coming to Judgment. among his Saints & throwing off the Temporal that the Eternal might be Establishd. (2008: 555)

Raine explains: 'Whereas for Locke mind is the passive mirror of a mechanized nature, for Blake Imagination is both Person and "place" where all beings and events are situated'; in Blake's understanding, 'it is by identifying "the true Man" with his mortal body that an understanding and knowledge of immortality has been lost': 'We must remember at all times that a "world" for Blake is situated not in Cartesian space but in consciousness; therefore every change of consciousness changes the world' (1991: 15, 17 and 18). Stevens' 'room', at once within 'Final Soliloquy' and that poem itself as it unfolds 'out of the central mind', provides room enough for that 'force capable of bringing about fluctuations in reality'. The stanzas of Stevens' poem are rooms in what Blake calls the 'world of Imagination', for 'In my Fathers house are many mansions' (John 14. 2), or, literally speaking, places 'In which we rest'.

In the middle of *Biographia Literaria*, Coleridge also says in his own way, 'God and the imagination are one', while making a distinction between two degrees of this force:

> The IMAGINATION then I consider either as primary, or secondary. The primary IMAGINATION I hold to be the living Power and prime Agent of all human Perception, and as a repetition in the finite mind of the eternal act of creation in the infinite I AM. The secondary I consider as an echo of the former, co-existing with the conscious will, yet still as identical with the primary in the *kind* of its agency, and differing only in *degree*, and in the *mode* of its operation. (1983: 1. 304)

If you take the primary imagination to be 'normal perception that produces the usual world of the senses' (Richards 1934: 58), then you are ignoring Coleridge's 'extraordinary use of language' in his definition:

> Jehovah named himself to Moses in Exodus as I AM; to do so was creative because self-consciousness implies the existence of something beyond the self, and as God's thoughts are acts, that which is implied is necessarily created. This process, eternal because an infinite being is not subject to time, is repeated within the finite human mind, and constitutes the primary imagination. (Jonathan Wordsworth 1984: 84 and 85)

What does Coleridge mean by the word 'repetition'? For Kierkegaard, 'repetition is a task for freedom... it signifies freedom itself, consciousness raised to the second power' (1983: 324):

> Approached from the side of a self becoming itself, a task for freedom is a task for self. A self's task is increasing its freedom, increasing its openness toward the possibility of repetition... But as one moves toward the religious or wondrous, one becomes less an actor than an alert receptor... Self and world become reciprocally articulate. (Hannay 1998: 294)

For Coleridge, the secondary imagination 'dissolves, diffuses, dissipates, in order to recreate; or where this process is rendered impossible, yet still at all events it struggles to idealise and to unify. It is essentially *vital*, even as all objects (*as* objects) are essentially fixed and dead' (1983: 1. 304). We could argue that 'The "secondary" imagination is basically the creative or poetic imagination' (Coleridge 1983: 1. lxxxix): 'the poet for Coleridge is a prophet'; his task is 'immensely important' (Jonathan Wordsworth 1984: 86), 'To carry the feelings of childhood into the powers of manhood' (Coleridge 1983: 1. 80-1), in order to 'lead you in at Heavens gate, | Built in Jerusalems wall' (Blake 2008: 231), but the poet's role 'is secondary, an echo, because it consists in giving form to the apprehension of God, not in the apprehension itself; and because it is conscious' (Jonathan Wordsworth 1984: 86).

What is primary becomes secondary in order to know itself: Since '*God wanted to become man, and still wants to*' (Jung 1984: 153), 'Love has pitched his mansion in | The place of excrement' (Yeats 1950: 295): He is now forgetfully sleepwalking in human consciousness. Poetry can awaken man's consciousness to feel that he is greater than he knows: 'We begin with the I KNOW MYSELF, in order to end with the absolute I AM' (Coleridge 1983: 1. 283). Our greatest poems contain Coleridge's 'border hope' (Jonathan Wordsworth 1984: 86) that 'We proceed from the SELF, in order to lose and find all self in GOD' (Coleridge 1983: 1. 283). When the divine imagination in man is wedded to the Muse in a true poet's stanzas, as immortal spirit is incarnated in the world of nature, a force conceals itself in the form of language, in 'the obscurity of an order', to change the world or the appearance of reality. Then 'Self and world become reciprocally articulate'.

Wordsworth and Coleridge had clearly been talking about the creative imagination in the early 1800s, for Wordsworth also articulates this divine force in man at the climax to the *1805 Prelude*. In Book XIII Wordsworth relates how, in 1793, on one of his walking 'excursions' 'with a youthful Friend', they 'Rouz'd up the Shepherd, who by ancient right | Of office is the Stranger's usual guide', in the middle of a 'glaring' night, 'to see the sun | Rise from the top of Snowdon' (XIII. 1-9):

With forehead bent
Earthward, as if in opposition set
Against an enemy, I panted up
With eager pace, and no less eager thoughts.
Thus might we wear perhaps an hour away,
Ascending at loose distance each from each,
And I, as chanced, the foremost of the Band;

When at my feet the ground appear'd to brighten,
And with a step or two seem'd brighter still;
Nor had I time to ask the cause of this,
For instantly a Light upon the turf
Fell like a flash: I looked about, and lo!
The Moon stood naked in the Heavens, at height
Immense above my head, and on the shore
I found myself of a huge sea of mist,
Which, meek and silent, rested at my feet[.] (XIII. 29-44)

With gentle and affectionate mockery, Wordsworth puts his younger self on a natural version of 'the time-honoured *Scala Perfectionis* of mysticism' (Bayley 1912: 1. 32). Near the top, he is afforded a vision of the 'Goddess of Complete Being': like that of Isis revealed to Apuleius' ass, she appears as a full moon above the sea. Except the sea, in Wordsworth's account, is of mist: 'and on the shore | I found myself of a huge sea of mist'; the reversed word order lends grandeur to the poet's account only to take it away, for his younger self does not come to self-knowledge on the shore, as we think momentarily when we read the lines through, but only discovers that he is standing on a sea of mist. Clearer self-knowledge comes much later with his writing up of the experience in verse. All the same, from the mountain's side, now the 'shore' of this sea of mist,

At distance not the third part of a mile
Was a blue chasm; a fracture in the vapour,
A deep and gloomy breathing-place through which
Mounted the roar of waters, torrents, streams
Innumerable, roaring with one voice. (*1805*, xiii. 55-9)

Something in the distance will lead eventually to greater self-knowledge. For Wordsworth also remembers how he brooded on this scene after it was presented to him:

A meditation rose in me that night
Upon the lonely Mountain when the scene
Had pass'd away, and it appear'd to me
The perfect image of a mighty Mind,
Of one that feeds upon infinity,
That is exalted by an underpresence,
The sense of God, or whatsoe'er is dim
Or vast in its own being[.] (*1805*, xiii. 66-73)

As Stevens says of 'a man in black space' in 'Metaphor as Degeneration', Wordsworth is 'Brooding sounds of river noises' as he recounts this significant spot of time on the side of Snowdon; 'And these images, these reverberations, | And others make certain how being | Includes death and the imagination' (1954: 444).

That which Wordsworth's younger self hears, 'the roar of waters, torrents, streams | Innumerable, roaring with one voice', comes to signify the undercurrent of perennial wisdom resurfacing in his imagination; that which Stevens calls, 'The swarthy water | That flows round the earth and through the skies, | Twisting among the universal spaces' (1954: 444). Like 'the waters' that race under the window-ledge of Yeats's tower, it is the nature of this stream to 'Run underground' again, despite its intermittent appearances in our greatest poetry (1950: 275). Acknowledging this quality of wisdom, as it emerges again in his own work, Stevens addresses his second self, his future poet-readers, in the penultimate poem of his *Collected Poems*, 'The River of Rivers in Connecticut'. As he does so, the poet echoes John Hemminge and Henry Condell's command 'To the Great Variety of Readers' of Shakespeare's *First Folio* to 'Reade him, therefore; and againe, and againe', and we feel that 'Deepe calleth unto deepe at the noyse of thy water-spouts: all thy waves, and thy billowes are gone over me' (Psalm 42. 7):

Call it, once more, a river, an unnamed flowing,

Space-filled, reflecting the seasons, the folk-lore
Of each of the senses; call it, again and again,
The river that flows nowhere, like a sea. (1954: 533)

This 'sea', emblem of 'a new heaven, and a new earth' (Revelation 21. 1) on earth, or eternity already apprehended in time and space, is taken up beautifully and paronomastically in the next and last poem of Stevens' *Collected Poems*, 'Not Ideas about the Thing but the Thing Itself', by 'A chorister whose c preceded the choir'. The sea into which the river of rivers flows, or doesn't flow, becomes a letter signifying a note; the undercurrent of wisdom that we have been tracing is at last transmuted into the scrawny cry of a bird that 'Seemed like a sound in his mind', heralding the future in man today:

It was part of the colossal sun,

Surrounded by its choral rings,
Still far away. It was like
A new knowledge of reality. (1954: 534)

Blake understood that 'whenever any Individual Rejects Error & Embraces Truth a Last Judgment passes upon that Individual', '& its Vision is seen by the [*Imaginative Eye*] of Every one according to the situation he holds' (2008: 562 and 554). Stevens ends his *Collected Poems* with a cry like 'A new knowledge' of such a second coming, apocalyptically 'still far away', 'yet close enough to wake | The chords above your bed to-night' (Stevens 1990: 132). In Stevens, as in Blake, 'What is under consideration is an event whose nature is rather a subtle change of awareness than a temporal fact' (Raine 1991: 79): 'the gathering of essential being' (Heidegger 1971: 176-7). Has any poet coming after Stevens managed to strike such a 'c' to tune the choir?

Epilogue

Should T. S. Eliot condescend to make his visit from his version of Purgatory, falling in with my step, 'In the uncertain hour before the morning | Near the ending of interminable night | At the recurrent end of the unending' (1969: 193), I am sure that his uncompounded ghost would find my conversation 'heretical' (1934: 24). But I am equally sure that part of his time in Purgatory involves the compounding of his soul back into the spirit of poetry that we have been tracing in this book in its various manifestations across the generations. This compounding of the poet with other souls in the afterlife, which Yeats also foresaw for himself in his penultimate poem 'Cuchulain Comforted', was a process that began, in fact, in Eliot's poetry, allusively, before the poet died, despite his best intentions, and proving the limitations of his old-fashioned religious orthodoxy. For his poems are full of the very supernatural powers that he would exorcise from our poetic tradition: they reside in the echoes we hear in his verse of the very poets he reproved.

In *Four Quartets* Eliot recounts how just before dawn:

While the dead leaves still rattled on like tin
Over the asphalt where no other sound was
Between three districts whence the smoke arose
I met one walking, loitering and hurried
As if blown towards me like the metal leaves
Before the urban dawn wind unresisting.
And as I fixed upon the down-turned face
That pointed scrutiny with which we challenge
The first-met stranger in the waning dusk
I caught the sudden look of some dead master
Whom I had known, forgotten, half recalled
Both one and many; in the brown baked features

The eyes of a familiar compound ghost
Both intimate and unidentifiable. (1969: 193)

Such a ghost is compounded perhaps of all the great poets of our western tradition from Homer to Dante to Yeats. But the most prominent among them is the one whose ideas Eliot found most 'repellent' (1987: 89): Shelley. In his unfinished final poem, 'The Triumph of Life', Shelley recounts a dawn vision that informs Eliot's 'familiar compound ghost', the many-in-one and the one-in-many:

Methought I sate beside a public way

Thick strewn with summer dust, and a great stream
Of people there was hurrying to and fro
Numerous as gnats upon the evening gleam,

All hastening onward, yet none seemed to know
Whither he went, or whence he came, or why
He made one of the multitude, yet so

Was borne amid the crowd as through the sky
One of the million leaves of summer's bier. –
Old age and youth, manhood and infancy,

Mixed in one mighty torrent did appear,
Some flying from the thing they feared and some
Seeking the object of another's fear,

And others as with steps toward the tomb
Pored on the trodden worms that crawled beneath,
And others mournfully within the gloom

Of their own shadow walked, and called it death... (2003: 605)

Eliot thought of 'Romantic' poets like Wordsworth and Shelley as belonging with 'the numbers of the great heretics of all time' (1987: 99 and 100) and that the younger Yeats's '"supernatural world" was the wrong supernatural world':

> It was not a world of spiritual significance, not a world of real Good and Evil, of holiness or sin, but a highly sophisticated lower mythology summoned, like a physician, to supply the fading pulse of poetry with some transient stimulant so that the dying patient may utter his last words. (1934: 46)

Unlike 'historical-materialist' critics today, 'Eliot's point is not to dismiss talk of the spirit as mumbo-jumbo, but rather to take it seriously'. Among modern critics, therefore, he may well offer the most significant resistance to my arguments concerning the supernatural in this book. As Justin Quinn summarizes:

> Most people will find talk of hierophants and heretics in the twentieth century comical, but Eliot, like Yeats, ignores the ironic guffaws. In different cultures, spiritual knowledge has been guarded by priest figures... who were trained in a discipline and as part of a tradition. The romantic poets, seeking to grasp this same knowledge, are trained only in rhymes and rhythms. It hardly seems enough. (2013: 112)

Eliot's major problem with this book would have been due to his critical position as a Christian. Such a standpoint led him ultimately to admit, even as a poet in *Four Quartets*, that 'The poetry does not matter' (1969: 179). He believed:

> Literary criticism should be completed by criticism from a definite ethical and theological standpoint. In so far as in any age there is common agreement on ethical and theological matters, so far can literary criticism be substantive. In ages

> like our own, in which there is no such common agreement, it is the more necessary for Christian readers to scrutinize their reading, especially of works of imagination, with explicit ethical and theological standards. (1986: 388)

I do agree with Eliot that poets should be very careful about the supernatural forces that their works invoke, as Chapter 2 of this book has hopefully demonstrated, and as Upton has acknowledged: 'Poetry has always been related to magic, and this is precisely why, in a place and time where the reality of God has begun to fade in the minds of the people, the art of poetry is always in danger of becoming satanic' (2008: 130). But I find that Eliot's orthodoxy ultimately inhibits him as a poet although it gives him license to censure other poets as a critic. What he says about the heretics Wordsworth and Shelley could almost be applied to his own work: 'They would not have been as great as they were but for the limitations which prevented them from being greater than they were' (1987: 100). According to Blake's version of the 'Last Judgment', Eliot should be 'Cast away' for troubling poetry and 'Religion with questions concerning Good & Evil' (2008: 554).

In fact, Eliot's own poetry undermines his Christian critical standing. As Michael O'Neill has astutely observed of *Four Quartets*:

> The poem values imaginative experience, but seeks to discipline it in the light of Christian belief, as though it, too, might otherwise exist only as something 'Driven by daemonic, chthonic | Powers'. Yet those 'Powers', picked out for emphasis, have their full share of the poetic spotlight, and Eliot seems less haply self-divided than powerfully able to peer into the very hiding places of Romanticism's appeal, taking Romanticism to be one domain in which 'daemonic, chthonic | Powers' are allowed expression. (2007: 80)

Eliot's orthodoxy does not contain such 'Powers' as might Blake's, or Yeats's or Stevens', apprehension of our divine imagination at work in poems. Therefore, Eliot's orthodoxy as a Christian critic does not prevent his poetry from becoming at least fascinated by the 'satanic' and I sense that he is sometimes 'flying from the thing [he] feared' and sometimes 'Seeking the object of another's fear' in his poems. On the other hand, Blake's radical brand of Protestantism saves him from demonic possession by comprehending those elves and ghosts as merely 'Weake Masters' (*The Tempest*, V. i. 41).

Raine understood that 'Between Eliot and Yeats lies a watershed of civilisation' (1999: 30):

> Eliot placed himself within the Western cultural and religious tradition with its emphasis on faith and morality. Yeats throughout his life followed the path of spiritual enlightenment, the goal to which religions are themselves at best only ways and means. Yeats's early master, Blake, had written that 'all religions are one' and that one religion he calls 'the religion of Jesus', which of course is not the Church but the religion of the Imagination, wisdom itself, the 'perennial philosophy'. (1999: 32)

Like Yeats, this book sees our future, 'not in terms of Christendom with its historical and religious context, its bent towards materialism and the secular and scientific culture which has been its outcome' (Raine 1999: 31), but in terms of that philosophy 'coeval with the universe itself' (Taylor 1969: 345), which comprehends Christianity as well as '"Oriental" religions' (Raine 1999: 31). My heretical belief is that the vagabond or 'ever wandering spirit of poetry', which I have attempted to trace in this book 'through its various metempsychoses' (see Coleridge 1849: 1. 31-2), and which conversed with 'Eternal Wisdom', 'Before the Hills appeerd, or Fountain flow'd' (*Paradise Lost*, VII.

8), has an integral role to play in that future. Sometimes neglected like a beggar, like wisdom herself today, at the gates of our cities and at the doors to our homes, we need now more than ever to listen to such 'Celestial Song' (*Paradise Lost*, VII. 12).

One of my mantras in this book is: 'We say God and the imagination are one' (Stevens 1954: 524). O'Neill notes that '"We say" is a phrase which reminds us that our words are sounds that will end like any other; our candles light up an immense darkness' (2007: 33). Stevens knows that words, 'like fish, or leaves, or birds' (Upton 2008: 135), are transient things made by God and that they can help each of us to 'feel that we are greater than we know' (Wordsworth 2009: 3. 363). By carefully finding, for a moment or an age or our future, the right words and putting them in their proper order, a poet can make language perform significant work for us in the world: because God is awakened in the hearts of receptive readers of great poems, which 'By indirections finde directions out' (*Hamlet*, II. i. 66), the poet taking dictation from 'the more than human "It"... which speaks whenever man speaks' (Caputo 1987: 290), 'Writing poetry – doing art – is integral to soul remaking, to mending inner nature' (Healy 2011: 182). Poetry does matter because it opens paths to self-knowledge by acknowledging indirectly and formally that which I had better call 'The bright eternal Self that is everywhere'; 'that is immortality, that is Spirit, that is all' (Yeats and Swami 1970: 135).

Bibliography

Agrippa, Henry Cornelius (2004) *Three Books of Occult Philosophy*, ed. Donald Tyson and trans. James Freake (St Paul: Llewellyn Publications).

Akenside, Mark (2000) *The Pleasures of Imagination*, ed. Jonathan Wordsworth (Otley: Woodstock Books).

Apuleius (1964) *The Golden Ass*, trans. Robert Graves (Harmondsworth: Penguin).

Aquinas, Thomas (1964) *Summa theologiæ*, trans. Thomas Gilby, 61 vols (London: Eyre and Spottiswoode).

Arnold, Matthew (1929) *Poetical Works* (London: Macmillan).

Augustine (2002) *Confessions*, trans. William Watts, 2 vols (Cambridge: Harvard University Press).

Avalon, Arthur (Sir John Woodroffe) (2008) *Shakti and Shakta* (Charleston: BiblioBazaar).

Babb, Lawrence (1940) 'The Background of "Il Penseroso"', *Studies in Philology*, 37: 257-73.
(1951) *The Elizabethan Malady* (East Lansing: Michigan State College Press).

Bate, Jonathan (1989) *Shakespeare and the English Romantic Imagination* (Oxford: Oxford University Press).
(1994) *Shakespeare and Ovid* (Oxford: Oxford University Press).
(2009) *Soul of the Age* (London: Penguin).

Bayley, Harold (1912) *The Lost Language of Symbolism*, 2 vols (London: Williams and Norgate).

Beckett, Samuel (1990) *The Complete Dramatic Works* (London: Faber and Faber).

Beckham, Victoria (2002) *Learning to Fly* (London: Penguin).

The Bible (2007) The Geneva Bible: 1560 Edition (Peabody: Hendrickson).
(2009) Matthew's Bible: 1537 Edition (Peabody: Hendrickson).
(2010) King James Version: 1611 Edition (Peabody: Hendrickson).

Blake, William (2002) *Collected Poems*, ed. W. B. Yeats (London: Routledge).
(2004) *The Complete Illuminated Books* (London: Thames and Hudson).
- (2008) *The Complete Poetry & Prose*, ed. David V. Erdman (Berkeley: University of California Press).

Blanchot, Maurice (1992) *The Sirens' Song*, trans. Gabriel Josipovici (Brighton: Harvester).

Bloom, Harold (1999) *Shakespeare: The Invention of the Human* (London: Fourth Estate).

Boethius (2003) *Theological Tractates, The Consolation of Philosophy*, trans. S. J. Tester et al. (Cambridge: Harvard University Press).

Bright, Timothie (1586) *A Treatise of Melancholie* (London: John Windet).

Brown, Terence (1999) *The Life of W. B. Yeats* (Oxford: Blackwell).

Browning, Robert (1940) *The Poetical Works* (Oxford: Oxford University Press).

Bundy, Murray (1952) '*The Elizabethan Malady: a Study of Melancholia in English Literature from 1580 to 1642.* By Lawrence Babb' (Review), *Shakespeare Quarterly*, 3: 275-278.

Burton, Robert (1621) *The Anatomy of Melancholy* (Oxford: Henry Cripps).

Bushrui, Suheil (2008) *Kahlil Gibran* (Oxford: Oneworld).

Cain, Thomas (1971) 'Spenser and the Renaissance Orpheus', *University of Toronto Quarterly*, 41: 24-47.

Campbell, Joseph (1993) *The Hero With a Thousand Faces* (London: Fontana).

Caputo, John (1987) *Radical Hermeneutics* (Indianapolis: Indiana University Press).

Carruthers, Mary (2008) *The Book of Memory* (Cambridge: Cambridge University Press).

Carver, Robert (2007) *The Protean Ass* (Oxford: Oxford University Press).

Chevalier, Jean and Alain Gheerbrant (1996) *Dictionary of Symbols*, trans. John Buchanan Brown (London: Penguin).

Clark, Timothy (1992) *Derrida, Heidegger, Blanchot* (Cambridge: Cambridge University Press).

Clarke, Edward (2012) *The Later Affluence of W. B. Yeats and*

Wallace Stevens (Basingstoke: Palgrave Macmillan).

Coleridge, Samuel Taylor (1849) *Notes and Lectures upon Shakespeare*, ed. H. N. Coleridge, 2 vols (London: William Pickering).
(1983) *Biographia Literaria*, ed. James Engell and W. Jackson Bate, 2 vols (Princeton: Princeton University Press).
(2001) *Poetical Works*, ed. J. C. C. Mays, 3 vols (Princeton: Princeton University Press).

Copenhaver, Brian (ed.) (2000) *Hermetica* (Cambridge: Cambridge University Press).

Cowper, William (1971) *Poetical Works*, ed. H. S. Milford and rev. Norma Russell (Oxford: Oxford University Press).

Curtius, Ernst Robert (1990) *European Literature and the Latin Middle Ages*, trans. Willard Trask (Princeton: Princeton University Press).

Dante (1996-2011) *The Divine Comedy of Dante Alighieri*, ed. and trans. Robert Durling, 3 vols (Oxford: Oxford University Press).
(1920) *Dantis Alagherii epistolae. The letters of Dante*, ed. and trans. Paget Toynbee (Oxford: Clarendon Press).

de Selincourt, Ernest (ed.) (1967) *The Letters of William and Dorothy Wordsworth: The Early Years*, rev. Chester Shaver (Oxford: Oxford University Press).

Donne, John (1996) *The Complete English Poems*. ed. A. J. Smith (London: Penguin).
(1990) *John Donne*, ed. John Carey (Oxford: Oxford University Press).

(1991) *The Complete English Poems*, ed. C. A. Patrides (London: Everyman).

Eliade, Mircea (2004) *Shamanism* (Princeton: Princeton University Press).

Eliot, T. S. (1934) *After Strange Gods* (London: Faber and Faber).
(1969) *The Complete Poems and Plays* (London: Faber and Faber).
(1986) *Selected Essays* (London: Faber and Faber).
(1987) *The Use of Poetry and the Use of Criticism* (London: Faber and Faber).

Fernie, Ewan (ed.) (2005) *Spiritual Shakespeares* (London: Routledge).

Fisch, Harold (1999) *The Biblical Presence in Shakespeare, Milton, and Blake* (Oxford: Oxford University Press).

Fish, Stanley (1972) *Self-Consuming Artifacts* (Berkeley: University of California Press).

Goddard, Harold (1960) *The Meaning of Shakespeare*, 2 vols (Chicago: University of Chicago Press).

Graves, Robert (1999) *The White Goddess*, ed. Grevel Lindop (London: Faber and Faber).

Gray, Thomas, William Collins and Oliver Goldsmith (1976) *Poems*, ed. Roger Lonsdale (London: Longman).

Greenblatt, Stephen (ed.) (2006) *The Norton Anthology of English Literature*, 2 vols (New York: Norton).

Hall, Manly (2003) *The Secret Teachings of All Ages* (New York: Penguin).

Hamilton, A. C. (ed.) (1997) *The Spenser Encyclopedia* (Toronto: University of Toronto Press).

Hanh, Thich Nhat (1991) *The Miracle of Mindfulness* (London: Rider).

Hartman, Geoffrey (ed.) (1972) *New Perspectives on Coleridge and Wordsworth* (New York: Columbia University Press).

Hazlitt, William (1982) *Selected Writings*, ed. Ronald Blythe (Harmondsworth: Penguin).

Healy, Margaret (2011) *Shakespeare, Alchemy and the Creative Imagination* (Cambridge: Cambridge University Press).

Heaney, Seamus (2001) *Electric Light* (London: Faber and Faber).

Heidegger (1971) *On the Way to Language*, trans. Peter Hertz (San Francisco: Harper).
(2004) *The Essence of Truth*, trans. Ted Sadler (London: Continuum).
(2007) *Unterwegs zur Sprache* (Stuttgart: Klett-Cotta).

Herbert, George (1978) *The Works*, ed. F. E. Hutchinson (Oxford: Oxford University Press).

Hesiod (2006-7) *Theogony, Works and Days, Testimonia, The Shield, Catalogue of Women, Other Fragments*, ed. and trans. Glenn Most, 2 vols (Cambridge: Harvard University Press).

Hillman, James and Michael Ventura (1993) *We've Had a Hundred Years of Psychotherapy – And the World's Getting Worse* (New York: HarperCollins).

Homer (2003) *The Odyssey*, trans. E. V. Rieu and D. C. H. Rieu (London: Penguin).

Hopkins, Gerard Manley (2002) *The Major Works*, ed. Catherine Phillips (Oxford: Oxford University Press).

Hughes, Ted (1993) *Shakespeare and the Goddess of Complete Being* (London: Faber and Faber).

Johnson, Samuel (2000) *The Major Works*, ed. Donald Greene (Oxford: Oxford University Press).

Jung, C. G. (1987) *Answer to Job* (London: Routledge).

Keats, John (2002) *Selected Letters*, ed. Robert Gittings and Jon Mee (Oxford: Oxford University Press).

Kierkegaard, Søren (1983) *Fear and Trembling, Repetition*, ed. and trans. Howard and Edna Hong (Princeton: Princeton University Press).

(1998) *The Point of View*, ed. and trans. Howard and Edna Hong (Princeton: Princeton University Press).

Kundera, Milan (1996) *Slowness*, trans. Linda Asher (London: Faber and Faber).

Lau, D. C. (trans.) (2001) *Tao Te Ching* (Hong Kong: Chinese University Press).

Macrobius (1952) *Commentary on the Dream of Scipio*, trans. W. H. Stahl (New York: Columbia University Press).

Marvell, Andrew (1971) *The Poems and Letters*, ed. H. M. Margoliouth, rev. Pierre Legouis, 2 vols (Oxford: Oxford

University Press).

Marx, Steven (2000) *Shakespeare and the Bible* (Oxford: Oxford University Press).

Milton, John (1972) *Poems Reproduced in Facsimile from the Manuscript in Trinity College, Cambridge* (Menston: Scolar Press).
(1998) *Milton: Paradise Lost,* ed. Alastair Fowler (London: Longman).
(2007a) *The Complete Shorter Poems,* ed. John Carey (Harlow: Pearson).
(2007b) *Paradise Lost,* ed. Barbara Lewalski (Oxford: Wiley-Blackwell).
(2009) *Complete Shorter Poems,* ed. Stella Revard (Oxford: Wiley-Blackwell).

Moore, W. W. (2000) *Points of View* (Oxford: Oxford University Press).

Morris, Tim (2013) '*The Later Affluence of W. B. Yeats and Wallace Stevens* by Edward Clarke' (Review), *The Modern Language Review,* 108: 638-9.

Muir, Edwin (1984) *Collected Poems* (London: Faber and Faber).

Nuttall, A. D. (2007) *Shakespeare the Thinker* (New Haven: Yale University Press).

O'Neill, Michael (2007) *The All-Sustaining Air* (Oxford: Oxford University Press).

O'Toole, Fintan (2002) *Shakespeare Is Hard, But So Is Life* (London: Granta).

Ovid (1904) *Shakespeare's Ovid*, ed. W. H. D. Rouse and trans. Arthur Golding (London: De La More Press).

Oxford English Dictionary Online (2013) <http://www.oed.com> 13 May 2013 (Oxford University Press).

Palgrave, Francis (ed.) (1913) *The Golden Treasury* (London: Macmillan).

Palmer, A. H. (ed.) (1972) *The Life and Letters of Samuel Palmer* (London: Eric and Joan Stevens).

Plato (1997) *Complete Works*, ed. John Cooper (Indianapolis: Hackett).

Plotinus (1992) *The Enneads*, trans. Stephan MacKenna (New York: Larson).

Pope, Alexander (2005) *The Poems*, ed. John Butt (London: Routledge).

Proust, Marcel (1996) *In Search of Lost Time*, trans. C. K. Scott Moncrieff and Terence Kilmartin, rev. D. J. Enright, 6 vols (London: Vintage).

Pullman, Philip (2012) *Grimm Tales* (London: Penguin).

Quinn, Justin (2013) '*The Later Affluence of W. B. Yeats and Wallace Stevens* by Edward Clarke' (Review), *The Wallace Stevens Journal*, 37: 111-2.

Raine, Kathleen (1985) *Defending Ancient Springs* (Ipswich: Golgonooza Press).

(1991) *Golgonooza City of Imagination* (Ipswich: Golgonooza Press).

(1999) *W. B. Yeats and the Learning of the Imagination* (Ipswich: Golgonooza Press).
(2002) *Blake and Antiquity* (London: Routledge).

Reisner, Noam (2009) *Milton and the Ineffable* (Oxford: Oxford University Press).

Rilke, Rainer Maria (2011) *Letters to a Young Poet*, trans. Charlie Louth (London: Penguin).

Rochester, John Wilmot (2010) *The Poems*, ed. Keith Walker and Nicholas Fisher (Oxford: Wiley-Blackwell).

Roud, Steve and Julia Bishop (eds) (2012) *The New Penguin Book of English Folk Songs* (London: Penguin).

Rumi, Jalaluddin (2001) *Selected Poems from the Divan-e Shams-e Tabrizi*, trans. R. A. Nicholson (Bethesda: Ibex Publishers).

Shah, Idries (1977) *The Sufis* (London: Octagon).

Shakespeare, William (1891) *The Works of Shakespeare*, ed. William George Clark and William Aldis Wright, 'The Globe Edition' (London: Macmillan).
(1953) *The Complete Works*, ed. Herbert Farjeon, 4 vols (London: The Nonesuch Press).
(1978) *Shakespeare's Sonnets*, ed. Stephen Booth (New Haven: Yale University Press).
(1987) *The Tempest*, ed. Frank Kermode (London: Methuen).
(1999) *The Sonnets and A Lover's Complaint*, ed. John Kerrigan (London: Penguin).
(2002) *The Complete Sonnets and Poems*, ed. Colin Burrow (Oxford: Oxford University Press).
(2004) *King Lear*, ed. R. A. Foakes (London: Thomas Learning).

(2006) *The Winter's Tale*, ed. J. H. P. Pafford (London: Thomas Learning).
(2008) *A Midsummer Night's Dream*, ed. Peter Holland (Oxford: Oxford University Press).
(2010) *Shakespeare's Sonnets*, ed. Katherine Duncan-Jones (London: Bloomsbury).
(2012) *Shakespeare's Sonnets*, ed. Paul Hammond (Oxford: Oxford University Press).

Shantideva (2006) *The Way of the Bodhisattva*, trans. Padmakara Translation Group (Boston: Shambhala Publications).

Shelley, Percy Bysshe (2003) *The Major Works*, ed. Zachary Leader and Michael O'Neill (Oxford: Oxford University Press).

Sidney, Sir Philip (1962) *The Poems*, ed. William Ringler (Oxford: Oxford University Press).
(1968) *The Defence of Poesie* (Menston: Scolar).

Smart, Christopher (1990) *Selected Poems*, ed. Karina Williamson and Marcus Walsh (London: Penguin).

Spenser, Edmund (1912) *The Poetical Works*, ed. J. C. Smith and Ernest de Selincourt (Oxford: Oxford University Press).
(1989) *The Yale Edition of the Shorter Poems*, ed. William Oram et al. (New Haven: Yale University Press).

Stevens, Wallace (1954) *Collected Poems* (New York: Knopf).
(1960) *The Necessary Angel* (London: Faber and Faber).
(1990) *Opus Posthumous*, ed. Milton J. Bates (London: Faber and Faber).
(1996) *Letters*, ed. Holly Stevens (Berkeley: University of California Press).

Taylor, Thomas (1969) *Selected Writings*, ed. Kathleen Raine and George Mills Harper (Princeton: Princeton University Press).

Tennyson, Alfred Lord (1894) *The Works* (London: Macmillan).

Theocritus (2008) *Idylls*, trans. Anthony Verity (Oxford: Oxford University Press).

Thorsen, Nils (2011) *Longing for the End of All* <http://www.melancholiathemovie.com> 8 July 2013.

Trakl, Georg (2001) *Poems and Prose*, trans. Alexander Stillmark (London: Libris).

Upton, Charles (2008) *Folk Metaphysics* (San Rafael: Sophia Perennis).

Vaughan, Henry (1957) *The Works*, ed. L. C. Martin (Oxford: Oxford University Press).

Virgil (1999-2000) *Eclogues, Georgics, Aeneid*, trans. H. R. Fairclough, rev. G. P. Gould, 2 vols (Cambridge: Harvard University Press).

Wilde, Oscar (2003) *The Complete Works* (Glasgow: HarperCollins).

Wordsworth, Jonathan (1984) *The Borders of Vision* (Oxford: Oxford University Press).
(1991) *Ancestral Voices* (Poole: Woodstock).

Wordsworth, William (1928) *Wordsworth's Prelude*, ed. Ernest de Selincourt (Oxford: Oxford University Press).
(1977) *The Prelude, 1798-1799*, ed. Stephen Parrish (Ithaca: Cornell University Press).

(1979a) *The Ruined Cottage and The Pedlar*, ed. James Butler (Ithaca: Cornell University Press).
(1979b) *William Wordsworth: The Prelude*, ed. Jonathan Wordsworth, M. H. Abrams and Stephen Gill (New York: Norton).
(2000) *The Major Works*, ed. Stephen Gill (Oxford: Oxford University Press).
(2007) *The Fenwick Notes*, ed. Jared Curtis (Penrith: Humanities-Ebooks).
(2009) *The Poems*, ed. Jared Curtis, 3 vols (Penrith: Humanities-Ebooks).

Wroe, Nicholas (2006) 'Leading Light', *The Guardian* (25 November) <http://www.guardian.co.uk> 28 June 2013.

Yates, Frances (2001) *The Occult Philosophy in the Elizabethan Age* (London: Routledge).
(2002) *Giordano Bruno and the Hermetic Tradition* (London: Routledge).
(2012) *The Art of Memory* (London: Pimlico).

Yeats, W. B. (1950) *Collected Poems* (London: Macmillan).
(1959) *Mythologies* (London: Macmillan).
(1961) *Essays and Introductions* (London: Macmillan).
(1962) *A Vision* (London: Macmillan).
(1980) *Autobiographies* (London: Macmillan).
(1997) *Last Poems*, ed. James Pethica (Ithaca: Cornell University Press).

Yeats, W. B. and Shree Purohit Swami (trans.) (1970) *The Ten Principal Upanishads* (London: Faber and Faber).

Zinman, Ira (2009) *Shakespeare's Sonnets and the Bible* (Indiana: World Wisdom; Kindle Edition).

BOOKS

Iff Books is interested in ideas and reasoning. It publishes material on science, philosophy and law. Iff Books aims to work with authors and titles that augment our understanding of the human condition, society and civilisation, and the world or universe in which we live.

9781782793700